Sweet
Shawlettes

Sweet Shawlettes

25 Irresistible Patterns for Knitting Cowls, Capelets, and More

Jean Moss

PHOTOGRAPHS BY
ALEXANDRA GRABLEWSKI

The Taunton Press

Text © 2012 by Jean Moss
The right of Jean Moss to be identified as the author of this book has
been asserted in accordance with Article 6bis of the Berne Convention
Photographs © 2012 by Alexandra Grablewski
Illustrations © 2012 by The Taunton Press, Inc.
Charts & Schematics © 2012 by Jean Moss

The Taunton Press

The Taunton Press, Inc., 63 South Main Street,
PO Box 5506, Newtown, CT 06470-5506
e-mail: tp@taunton.com

Editor: ERICA SANDERS-FOEGE
Developmental editor: REBECCA BEHAN
Copy editor: BETTY CHRISTIANSEN
Indexer: BARBARA MORTENSON

Cover and interior design: ALISON WILKES
Layout: CATHY CASSIDY
Illustrator: JEAN MOSS and CHRISTINE ERIKSON
Photographer: ALEXANDRA GRABLEWSKI
Stylist: KIM FIELD
Hair and Makeup: NOELLE MARINELLI

The following names/manufacturers appearing in
Sweet Shawlettes are trademarks: Bergere de France®,
Berroco® Glacé™, Metallica FX®, Purelife®, Rowan®.
Standard Yarn Weight System (p. 124) and Needle and
Hook Sizing information (p. 127) courtesy of the Craft Yarn
Council, www.yarnstandards.com

Library of Congress Cataloging-in-Publication Data

Moss, Jean.
Sweet shawlettes : 25 irresistible patterns for knitting capelets, cowls, collars & more / Jean Moss.
    p. cm.
Includes index.
ISBN 978-1-60085-400-2
1. Knitting--Patterns. 2. Knit goods. I. Title.
TT825.M68326 2012
677'.028245--dc23
                        2011040013
Printed in the United States of America
10 9 8 7 6 5 4 3 2 1

Dedication

For Isabella, Ava, and Lyra
—my sweet shawlettes

Acknowledgments

Many talented people have been involved in the making of *Sweet Shawlettes*, and my grateful appreciation goes to them all, with special thanks to: Senior editor Erica Sanders-Foege at The Taunton Press for commissioning this book; Shawna Mullen for stepping in at the eleventh hour with patience and good humor; Rebecca Behan for her editing and helpful suggestions; Rowan Yarns and Sublime for the gorgeous fibers that shine through in every project; Vicky Sedgwick at Rowan Yarns for sending out the many sample yarns so efficiently; my trusty knitters Ann Banks, Mary Coe, Joan Crawford, Glennis Garnett, Jenny Metcalfe, and Rita Taylor, who tested the patterns and faithfully created every stitch; Alexandra Grablewski for bringing the shawlettes to life in her photographs; and to Philip Mercer for his, as ever, tireless and wide-ranging support.

Remembering Mary Coe, a lovely woman and ace knitter, who sadly died before this book was published.

Contents

Introduction

I'VE ALWAYS BEEN A DOER. I NEED TO MAKE THINGS WITH my hands—stitches, food, gardens, music—and so, for me, *Sweet Shawlettes* has been a dream project. From little more than a necklace to more substantial capelets, cowls, collars, furbelows, and fichus, the shawlette provides the ultimate opportunity to explore shape, stitch, color, and texture—all without the commitment a larger piece demands. And, as many use small quantities of yarn, these stash-busting designs are terrific for last-minute handmade gifts. If you, like me, have a tendency to buy tiny amounts of luxury yarns you just can't resist, but then wonder what on earth to do with them, well, problem solved—you'll find many options in *Sweet Shawlettes!*

My work as a handknit designer and, more recently, as tour host for adventurous knitters and fiber lovers involves a lot of travel. The portable shawlette is my ideal companion, something to occupy my needles whether exploring a Welsh mountain or a Moroccan kasbah. Since often there is no big deal about gauge—within reason of course—and sizing is less important, shawlettes also are perfect for new knitters.

With the 25 designs in this collection, a wonderful voyage of discovery started to unfold for me. I've arranged the designs into four chapters, each reflecting a different mood. In **Country**, you'll find shawlettes that look to nature for inspiration and use combinations of intarsia, lace,

cables, and appliqué. **Couture** is pure style, with in-your-face block color, shadow-knit stripes, and bold entrelac—guaranteed to get you noticed! **Folk** explores the nuts and bolts of the knitting tradition: Fair Isle, cables, lace, plaid, and patchwork, including new takes on old techniques, a lace Möbius, and a denim gansey design. **Vintage** is an ode to fabulous fashion through the ages—from Elizabethan neck ruffs and *Wuthering Heights* shawls, through the decadent style of Lord Byron, to the extravagant glitz and glamour of the 1950s screen goddesses.

Whether you are new to knitting or a lifelong devotee, the patterns in this book provide an opportunity to learn something new and create unique, beautiful designs.

The Importance of Fiber

Yarn is hugely important in any pattern. It's the vehicle for showcasing the stitches that we spend so long creating, so it has to be right for the job. I've had such fun picking the perfect fiber for each of these projects. The neck is a highly sensual area, so it's imperative that the yarn is soft and sumptuous, yet holds the correct shape and does the stitch justice. Some yarns, like cashmere, are beautiful enough in themselves and need only a stylish shape to create a wonderful design. Others with crisp stitch definition, such as cotton and linen, cry out for a cable or sculptured stitch, whilst painterly random-dyed yarns can effortlessly introduce exquisite color into a design.

The yarns I've chosen for this book reflect the unique nature of each design—some shawlettes work best with natural fibers, others with luxurious blends, and still others can take pretty much any yarn you care to cast on. I've tried to use yarns easily available through local yarn shops and online, but to make substitutions easy, I've included a fiber list on p. 122 and a Standard Yarn Weight System on p. 124 at the back of the book.

Shawlettes also provide the perfect opportunity to get creative with buttons, buckles, beads, and closures. These can make or break a project, so make sure you choose yours carefully. I love vintage style, so I try to recycle costume jewelry and yard sale treasures. After all, a shawlette featuring buttons from your grandmother's favorite jacket or an heirloom brooch is meaningful beyond just the stitchwork. Of course there are gorgeous new fasteners to be had, but remember that often the perfect bead, button, or buckle can be closer than you might think.

Knits have never been more important in the world of fashion. Beautifully crafted, sophisticated pieces expressing the wearer's personality represent the contemporary face of handknits. I hope this book will inspire you to knit my sweet shawlettes, either to flaunt flamboyantly or gift generously to friends and family.

—*Jean Moss*

CHAPTER 1

Country

WHEN I HAVEN'T GOT MY HEAD IN A PATTERN, YOU CAN BE SURE to find me in the garden. The plants are my stitch patterns, chosen for color or texture, the flowerbeds comprise the different shapes that make up the garment, and the paths are the seams that hold the design together.

Inspired by early morning in my Welsh garden, fresh with dew or frost and accompanied by the music of the dawn chorus, these designs look to nature but with a romantic, quirky slant. Beginner knitters will love **Garland**, a versatile piece that can double as a belt. **Green at Heart**, a straightforward lace and cable knit, uses recycled yarn. Try chasing away your lace demons with **Kardamili** or honing your intarsia with **Madame Alfred**. Conquer your fear of Fair Isle with the dramatic **Frost** choker, or personalize **Evergreen** with your own creative touches—work in moss stitch, rib, cable, and *ta-da*, a different scarf emerges!

The motifs are naïve, informed by antique samplers and botanical illustrations. Techniques showcased include intarsia, lace, Fair Isle, and appliqué, and there are single crochet, braid, and ruffle edgings.

Madame Alfred Shawlette

The heady scent of the climbing rose Madame Alfred Carrière heralds the start of summer in my garden. I wanted to convey a similar feeling of sensual overload when designing this piece—using color and pattern instead of fragrance. The lenpur linen drapes wonderfully, redolent of Madame's decadent noisette blossom. Combining intarsia and lace and finished with a frill, this pattern is for the experienced knitter, but I hope you'll agree it's well worth the effort!

SKILL LEVEL
Experienced

FINISHED MEASUREMENTS
62 in. (158 cm) wide, 21 in. (53.5 cm) long, including borders

YARN
Rowan® Lenpur Linen
126 yd. (115 m) per 50 g ball:
2 balls Creek 567 (A)
1 ball each Jungle 569 (B), Cocoa 573 (C),
Zest 564 (D), Vivid 563 (E),
and Lagoon 565 (F)
6 balls Saffron 561 (G)

NOTIONS
Size 6 U.S. (4 mm) extra-long circular
needle *or size to obtain gauge*
Size G-6 U.S. (4 mm) crochet hook
Tapestry needle

GAUGE
22 sts and 30 rows = 4 in. (10 cm) in
Rosebud Lace Chart pattern

TO MAKE SHAWLETTE
Using (G), cast on 45 sts.
Work the Rosebud Lace Chart back and forth on the needle and repeat all 20 rows, inc 1 st at both ends of every row, until there are 315 sts, keeping the chart pattern correct to the edges as you increase—135 rows. Work 5 more rows in pattern and then cast off loosely as follows: K1, *pass this st back to the LH needle and k2tog; rep from * across row.

Using (A) and starting at the left RS edge of the Shawlette, pick up and k 140 sts down the sloping side edge, 45 sts across the cast-on edge, and 140 sts up the other sloping side edge—325 sts.

Work 1 row.

Work all 16 rows of the Rosebud Intarsia Chart, inc 1 st at both ends of every alt row and centering the chart as follows:

RS rows Work the last 10 sts, work the 38-st repeat 8 times across the row, work the first 11 sts.

WS rows Work the last 11 sts, work the 38-st repeat 8 times across the row, work the first 10 sts.

Incorporate the extra sts into the pattern as you inc—341 sts.

Work 1 row in (A) and then change to (G) and work the frill:

Next row (WS) *P1, p1 into back and front of next st; rep from * across row, ending with p1.

continued on page 12

Next row *K2, k1 into front and back of next st; rep from * across row, ending with k1.
Next row *P3, p1 into back and front of next st; rep from * across row, ending with p1.
Cast off loosely as for the lace chart.

FINISHING
Securely weave ends into like colors.
Using the crochet hook and (G), with RS facing, work single crochet (p. 120) across the top of the Shawlette. Fasten off.

Madame Alfred Schematic

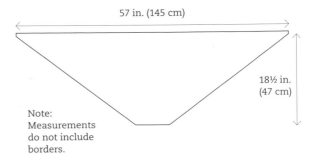

57 in. (145 cm)

18½ in. (47 cm)

Note: Measurements do not include borders.

Embellish this shawlette with a vintage brooch fastener (p. 10) or tuck the ends over your shoulders for a lovely, loose wrap.

Rosebud Intarsia Chart

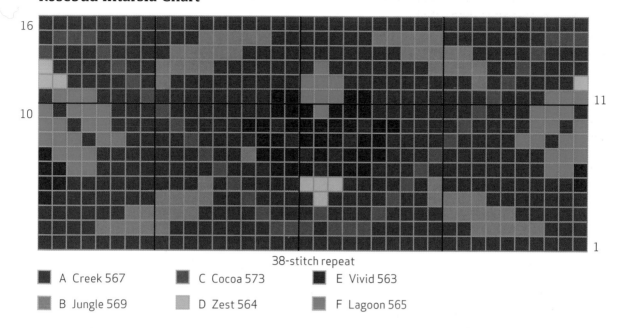

38-stitch repeat

■ A Creek 567 ■ C Cocoa 573 ■ E Vivid 563

■ B Jungle 569 ■ D Zest 564 ■ F Lagoon 565

Rosebud Lace Chart

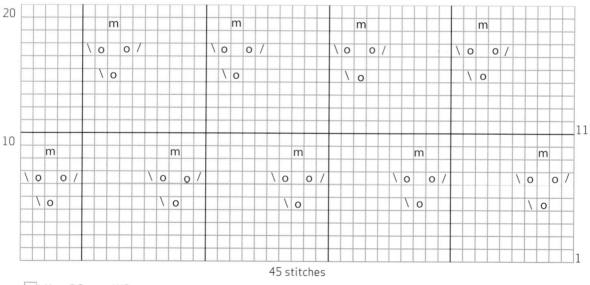

45 stitches

☐ K on RS, p on WS

o Yo

\ Ssk

/ K2tog

m Make knot—(K1, p1, k1, p1, k1, p1, k1) in st to make 7 sts, pass sts over the first st
one at a time, then pass first st to LH needle and knit into back of st.

Kardamili Shawlette

I often return from holidays in the Peloponnese bearing scarves bedecked with tiny flowers—my way of bringing home some Greek sun! This colorful piece, inspired by these souvenirs, evokes the ethos of Protomagia, the May Day festival of flowers in Greece. You can make your shawlette unique by choosing different flowers, colors, and beads to reflect your own style. The bamboo yarn has wonderful drape and the mesh pattern is easy to knit, making this a perfect starter project for aspiring lace knitters.

SKILL LEVEL
Intermediate

FINISHED MEASUREMENTS
54 in. (137 cm) wide, 24½ in. (62 cm) long when blocked

YARN
Sublime Bamboo & Pearls DK
104 yd. (95 m) per 50 g ball:
6 balls Saffron 212 (A)
1 ball Shantung 211 (B)

NOTIONS
1 pair size 6 U.S. (4 mm) needles
1 pair size 8 U.S. (5 mm) needles
or size to obtain gauge
Size G-6 U.S. (4 mm) crochet hook
Tapestry needle
Beading needle
25 pearl beads

GAUGE
17 sts and 22 rows = 4 in. (10 cm) in Mesh Stitch pattern

SPECIAL STITCHES
Mesh Stitch
Row 1 Purl.
Row 2 K1, *k1 through horizontal bar before next st, k1, pass made st over. Rep from * to the last st.

TO MAKE SHAWLETTE
Using size 8 U.S. (5 mm) needles and (A), cast on 3 sts and work in Mesh St. to the end.
At the same time inc as follows:
*1 st at both ends of every row 5 times, then on the following alt row once; rep this 7-row inc sequence until there are 231 sts, keeping the Mesh St. pattern correct. Work 1 row in pattern—134 rows.
Cast off loosely as follows: K1, *pass this st back to the LH needle and k2tog; rep from * across row.

Flower (Make 25)
Using size 6 U.S. (4 mm) needles and (A), cast on 35 sts.
Row 1 (WS) *K1, cast off 5 sts (2 sts on RH needle); rep from * to end—10 sts.
Run a threaded tapestry needle through the rem sts on needle, pull tight, and secure, leaving a long tail for attaching to Shawlette later. Sew 1 pearl bead to the center of the flower using the beading needle.

FINISHING (BORDER)
Pin to the finished dimensions and press lightly (p. 116) on the WS.
Using the crochet hook and (B), work a picot edge around all three sides of shawlette as follows:
Rows 1 and 2 Work single crochet (p. 120) around the edges of the Shawlette.
Row 3 Sl st into first ch, *ch 5, sl st into 4th chain from hook, ch 2, sk next 2 sts, 1 sl st into next st; rep from * around Shawlette.

continued on page 16

Using (A), attach flowers securely to picot knots on the sides labeled A and B on the schematic: 1 flower at each corner, plus 1 at center V, then approx every 4th picot point between. After attaching all 25 flowers, tightly wrap about ¼ in. (6 mm) of yarn (B) tightly around the base of each flower and secure by inserting the needle into the top of the wraps at the base of each flower and coming out of the center of the flower, and then cutting the yarn.

Kardamili Schematic

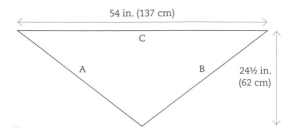

Little cultured pearls, recycled from a 1950s-era necklace, make the center of each flower (and reflect my passion for vintage jewelry).

Garland Necklet

Get a touch of Venetian pizzazz with this necklet of flowers—a versatile addition to any wardrobe. Although the yarn I've used came out of my stash, many other fancy yarns will do. This is a great project for knitting up a quick gift, with no fuss about gauge or yarns. Just find your own mix of texture, luster, and glitz, and get out there and sparkle!

SKILL LEVEL
Easy

FINISHED MEASUREMENTS
65 in. (165 cm) long

YARN
Colorway 1 (p. 20)
Bergere de France Tulle
172 yd. (160 m) per 50 g ball:
1 ball each Pink (A) and Green (C)
Rowan Mulberry Silk
164 yd. (150 m) per 50 g hank:
1 hank Magenta (B)
Berroco® Glacé
75 yd. (69 m) per 50 g hank:
1 hank 2846 (D)
Colinette Zanziba
103 yd. (94 m) per 100 g hank:
1 hank Bright Charcoal (E)

Colorway 2 (opposite)
Rowan Pure Silk DK
137 yd. (125 m) per 50 g ball:
1 ball Firefly 162 (A)
Louisa Harding Sari Ribbon
66 yd. (60 m) per 50 g ball:
1 ball Flame (B)
Berroco Metallic FX®
85 yd. (78 m) per 25 g hank:
1 hank Gold 1001 (C)

Rowan Shimmer
191 yd. (175 m) per 25 g ball:
1 ball Jet 95 (D)
Rowan Chunky Chenille
151 yd. (140 m) per 100 g ball:
1 ball Parchment 383 (E)
From my stash
Unlabeled viscose ribbon
1 ball Burgundy (F)

NOTIONS
1 pair size 3 U.S. (3.25 mm)
double-pointed needles for Colorway 1 (B)
and Colorway 2 (D)
1 pair size 6 U.S. (4 mm) double-pointed
needles for Colorway 2 (A)
1 pair size 8 U.S. (5 mm) double-pointed
needles for Colorway 1 (D) and Colorway 2 (C),
(E), and (F)
1 pair size 10 U.S. (7 mm) double-pointed
needles for Colorway 1 (A) and (C)
and Colorway 2 (E)
1 pair size 11 U.S. (8 mm) double-pointed
needles for Colorway 2 (B)
Tapestry needle

GAUGE
For once, gauge is not important!

continued on page 21

TO MAKE NECKLET

Work 2 lengths of I-cord (p. 119), one each in (C) and (D) to measure 65 in. (165 cm) when braided. To do this, make each cord slightly longer than the given length and then sew together at one end the 2 cords plus either 1 strand of (E), if using Colorway 1, or 3 strands of (E), if using Colorway 2. Braid the 3 strands until the correct length is achieved. Fasten off and sew together at the end to secure the braid.

For Colorway 1 (opposite)

Make 5 cabbage roses in (B) and 3 florets in (A).

For Colorway 2 (p. 19)

Make 3 cabbage roses in (F), 2 in (A), and 3 florets in (B).

Cabbage Rose

Cast on 10 sts.
Row 1 Knit.
Row 2 Purl.
Row 3 Knit in front and back of every stitch. To do so, knit the next st but do not take the st off LH needle. Knit the st again through the back loop and then slip the original st off LH needle—20 sts.
Row 4 Purl.
Row 5 Knit in front and back of every st—40 sts.
Row 6 Purl.
Row 7 Knit in front and back of every st—80 sts.
Row 8 Purl.
Cast off. Twist into a rose shape and secure with the end of knitting.

Florets

Loosely cast on 21 sts. Work 4 rows in Stockinette St. Pass all sts one at a time over the 1st st, then fasten off. Roll the cast-on edge into the cast-off edge by making 1 twist to form a floret, then sew into place.

FINISHING

Using the tapestry needle, neatly sew the finished pieces to the cord (D) at the following intervals, as shown on the schematic:
Sew 1 floret at each end.
Sew 1 rose about 5 in. (12.7 cm) from each end.
Then at one end only, beginning about 5 in. (12.7 cm) from the last sewn rose, sew 1 rose, 1 floret, and 2 more roses all evenly spaced about 5 in. (12.7 cm) apart.

Garland Schematic

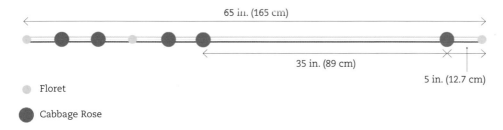

65 in. (165 cm)

35 in. (89 cm)

5 in. (12.7 cm)

● Floret

● Cabbage Rose

In colorway 2 (p. 19), a strand of jet yarn winds through the design and highlights the braided cord; in colorway 1 (opposite), a hint of pale green complements brilliant magenta and pale pink cabbage roses.

Green at Heart Collar

Wear your eco-heart on your sleeve with this cozy collar, knitted in recycled wool so you can rest easy you're not adding to your carbon footprint. The pattern mixes cables and lace for a satisfying weekend project—perfect for those who like to be both stylish and sustainable!

SKILL LEVEL
Intermediate

FINISHED MEASUREMENTS
8 in. (20 cm) wide, 34½ in. (87.5 cm) long

YARN
Rowan Purelife® Renew
82 yd. (75 m) per 50 g ball:
3 balls Digger 682

NOTIONS
1 pair size 10 U.S. (6 mm) needles
or size to obtain gauge
Cable needle
Tapestry needle
3 buttons

GAUGE
18 sts and 20 rows = 4 in. (10 cm) in
Green at Heart chart pattern (p. 25)

Note
Slip the first stitch and knit into the back of the last stitch on every row.

TO MAKE COLLAR
Cast on 38 sts and work in Moss St. for 1 in. (2.5 cm), ending on a WS row.
Buttonhole row (RS) Slip 1, k4, cast off 3 sts, k9, cast off 4 sts, k9, cast off 3 sts, k4, k1tbl.
Next row (WS) Work the Green at Heart Chart, starting on row 1, as follows:
Slip 1, work 36 sts of chart, k1tbl.
At the same time cast on over the cast-off sts when you come to them.
Work rows 1–19 of the chart in this manner, then rep from row 4 nine times (163 rows of chart); work row 1.
Work 1 in. (2.5 cm) in Moss St.
Cast off in pattern.

FINISHING
Weave in all ends securely using the tapestry needle.
Press lightly (p. 116) on the WS.
Attach 3 buttons opposite the buttonholes along the side edge of the Collar.

continued on page 25

Create a completely different look by changing just the buttons, or try a solid yarn for fabulous stitch definition.

Green at Heart Chart

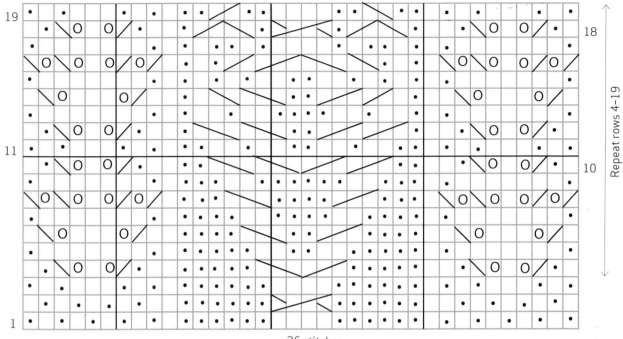

19 ... 18

11 ... 10

Repeat rows 4–19

1

36 stitches

Note: Chart starts on WS row.

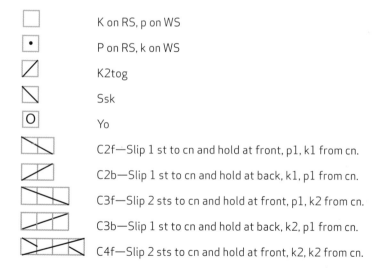

	K on RS, p on WS
•	P on RS, k on WS
/	K2tog
\	Ssk
O	Yo
	C2f—Slip 1 st to cn and hold at front, p1, k1 from cn.
	C2b—Slip 1 st to cn and hold at back, k1, p1 from cn.
	C3f—Slip 2 sts to cn and hold at front, p1, k2 from cn.
	C3b—Slip 1 st to cn and hold at back, k2, p1 from cn.
	C4f—Slip 2 sts to cn and hold at front, k2, k2 from cn.

Green at Heart Schematic

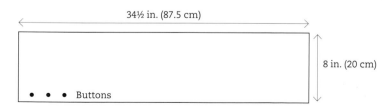

34½ in. (87.5 cm)

8 in. (20 cm)

• • • Buttons

Evergreen Scarf

This leafy scarf keeps you warm and stylish on the chilliest days, but the cashmerino yarn is light enough to take you through the spring, too. The bulk of the knitting is garter stitch, reversible, and stress-free. Make the scarf your own by playing around with variations on the leaves. Keep the stitchwork simple with just one type of leaf, or use all three patterns in different colors as I did. You could also try striping the garter stitch for a scarf as colorful as the leaves. The choice is yours!

SKILL LEVEL
Easy

FINISHED MEASUREMENTS
Small: 2 in. (5 cm) wide, 52 in. (132 cm) long
Large: 2 in. (5 cm) wide, 68 in. (173 cm) long

YARN
Rowan Cashsoft DK
126 yd. (115 m) per 50 g ball:
2 balls Lime 509 (A)
1 ball Spruce 541 (B)
1 ball Cashew 522 (C)

NOTIONS
1 pair size 6 U.S. (4 mm) needles
or size to obtain gauge
Size D-3 (3.25 mm) crochet hook
Stitch holder
Tapestry needle

GAUGE
24 sts and 48 rows = 4 in. (10 cm) in
Garter Stitch (p. 119)

Note
Slip the first stitch and knit into the back of the last stitch on every row to make a neat selvage.

TO MAKE SCARF
Fringe 1
Using (A) cast on 6 sts and, working in Garter St. throughout, cont until work measures 11½ in. (29 cm) ending on a WS row. Place stitches on the holder.

Fringe 2
Using (A), cast on 6 sts and, working in Garter St. throughout, cont until work measures 8½ in. (21.5 cm), ending on a WS row.
Next row (RS) Work across all 6 sts of Fringe 2, and then all 6 sts of Fringe 1—12 sts.
Cont until work measures 28 in. (71 cm) from the top of the fringes to make a scarf that wraps once around the neck, or 44 in. (112 cm) to make a scarf that wraps twice.
Cont to work the scarf as follows:
Work across the first 6 sts (Fringe 1), then join a new ball of yarn and work to the end (Fringe 2).
Working the 2 pieces separately, when Fringe 2 measures 8½ in. (21.5 cm), ending on a RS row, cast off.
Cont working Fringe 1 until the total length measures 11½ in. (29 cm), ending on a WS row. Cast off.

FINISHING
Using the tapestry needle, securely weave in ends.

continued on page 29

*Cross-pollinate
Evergreen with
Kardamili (p. 14) by
sprinkling a few of its
beaded flowers among
the leaves.*

Large Stockinette Stitch Leaf (Make 10)

Using (B), cast on 5 sts.

Row 1 (RS) K2, yo, k1, yo, k2—7 sts.

Row 2 (and all WS rows) Purl.

Row 3 K3, yo, k1, yo, k3—9 sts.

Row 5 K4, yo, k1, yo, k4—11 sts.

Row 7 Ssk, k7, k2tog—9 sts.

Row 9 Ssk, k5, k2tog—7 sts.

Row 11 Ssk, k3, k2tog—5 sts.

Row 13 Ssk, k1, k2tog—3 sts.

Row 15 Sl 1, k2tog, psso—1 st.

Fasten off rem st.

Small Stockinette Stitch Leaf (Make 8)

Using (C), cast on 5 sts.

Row 1 (RS) K2, yo, k1, yo, k2—7 sts.

Row 2 (and all WS rows) Purl.

Row 3 Ssk, k3, k2tog—5 sts.

Row 5 Ssk, k1, k2tog—3 sts.

Row 7 Sl 1, k2tog, psso—1 st.

Fasten off rem st.

Garter Stitch Leaf (Make 10)

Note: M1 by knitting into the st below the next st and, without slipping the made st off the needle, knit into next st.

Using (A), cast on 9 sts.

Row 1 K3, sl2tog kwise, k1, p2sso, k3—7 sts.

Row 2 K1, m1, k2, p1, k2, m1, k1—9 sts.

Row 3 K3, sl2tog kwise, k1, p2sso, k3—7 sts.

Row 4 K1, m1, k2, p1, k2, m1, k1—9 sts.

Row 5 K3, sl2tog kwise, k1, p2sso, k3—7 sts.

Row 6 K3, p1, k3.

Row 7 K2, sl2tog kwise, k1, p2sso, k2—5 sts.

Row 8 K2, p1, k2.

Row 9 K1, sl2tog kwise, k1, p2sso, k1—3 sts.

Row 10 K1, p1, k1.

Row 11 Sl2tog kwise, k1, p2sso—1 st.

Fasten off rem st.

Using the crochet hook, make 28 single crochet chains (see p. 120), each about 2 in. (5 cm) long. Attach one end of each chain to the Scarf and the other end to a leaf, as shown on the schematic.

Evergreen Schematic

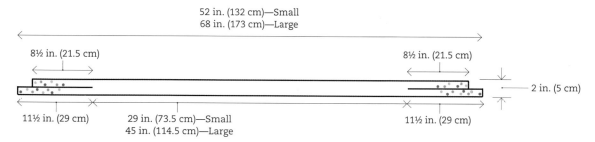

52 in. (132 cm)—Small
68 in. (173 cm)—Large

8½ in. (21.5 cm)

8½ in. (21.5 cm)

2 in. (5 cm)

11½ in. (29 cm)

29 in. (73.5 cm)—Small
45 in. (114.5 cm)—Large

11½ in. (29 cm)

- Garter Stitch Leaf in (A)

- Large Stockinette Stitch Leaf in (B)

- Small Stockinette Stitch Leaf in (C)

Frost Choker

I've always admired the Selbu knitting from Norway, which traditionally uses black-and-white patterning with a dash of scarlet. These dramatic colors occur in many cultures and are said to symbolize birth, life, and death. To complement this Nordic pattern, I've used vintage snowflake pewter buttons, but metal frog fasteners would work equally well. The glorious cashmerino yarn is super to knit with and so soft you'll hardly know you're wearing it—a chic and cozy choker to ward off the cold on winter walks in the country.

SKILL LEVEL
Intermediate

FINISHED MEASUREMENTS
Small: 14 in. (35.5 cm) wide,
4 in. (10 cm) long
Medium: 16 in. (40.5 cm) wide,
4 in. (10 cm) long
Large: 18 in. (45.7 cm) wide,
4 in. (10 cm) long
(Pattern is written for size Small, with Medium and Large instructions in parentheses where necessary.)

YARN
Rowan Cashsoft 4 Ply
175 yd. (160 m) per 50 g ball:
2 balls Black 422 (A)
2 balls Cream 433 (B)
1 ball Poppy 438 (C)

NOTIONS
1 pair size 3 U.S. (3.25 mm)
needles *or size to obtain gauge*
Tapestry needle
3 buttons

GAUGE
30 sts and 32 rows = 4 in. (10 cm) in Frost Chart pattern

Notes
Slip the first stitch and knit into the back of the last stitch on every row.
For information on knitting Fair Isle, see p. 118.

TO MAKE CHOKER
Using the Continental Cast-On (p. 118) and yarn (A), cast on 105 (119, 135) sts. Then join yarn (B) and work 3 rows of the Braid Pattern as follows:
Row 1 *K1 (A), k1 (B); rep from * to last st, k1 (A).
Row 2 Bring both colors to the back of the work. *K1 (A), k1 (B), always bringing the next color to be used **over** the top of the last color used. Rep from * to last st, k1 (A).
Row 3 Bring both colors to the front of the work. *P1 (A), p1 (B), always bringing the next color to be used **over** the top of the last color used. Rep from * to last st, k1 (A).
Purl 1 row in (A).
Work the 25 rows of the Frost Chart, setting the pattern as follows:
RS rows Work 7 sts in Moss St. (p. 119), work the last 9 (4, 0) sts of the chart, work 24 sts of the chart 3 (4, 5) times across each row, work the first 10 (5, 1) sts of the chart, work 7 sts in Moss St.
WS rows Work 7 sts in Moss St. work the last 10 (5, 1) sts of the chart, work 24 sts of the chart 3 (4, 5) times

continued on page 32

Frost Chart

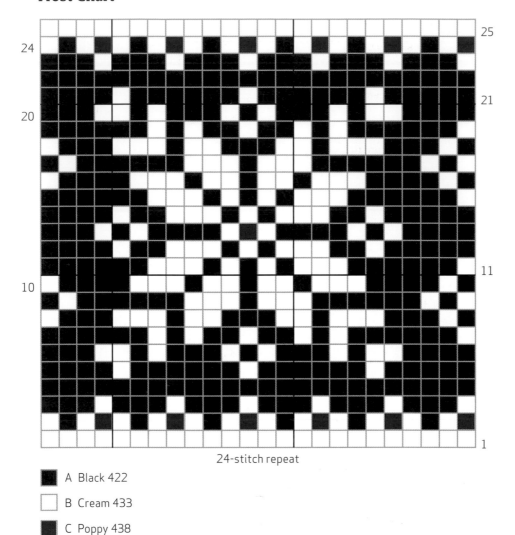

24-stitch repeat

■ A Black 422

□ B Cream 433

■ C Poppy 438

across each row, work the first 9 (4, 0) sts of the chart, work 7 sts in Moss St.

At the same time work buttonholes on rows 1, 2, 3, and 4 (first buttonhole), 11, 12, 13, and 14 (second buttonhole), and 21, 22, 23, and 24 (third buttonhole) as follows: Work 4 sts, turn and work a further 3 rows on these sts. Rejoin a new ball of yarn to rem sts and work 4 rows in the pattern. Work across all sts on the following row.

Purl 1 row in (A).
Work 3 rows of Braid Pattern as set, and cast off in (A).

FINISHING
Using the tapestry needle, securely weave in all ends.
Attach 3 buttons opposite the buttonholes along the other edge of the Choker.

Frost Schematic

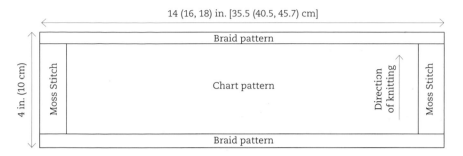

14 (16, 18) in. [35.5 (40.5, 45.7) cm]

	Braid pattern		
Moss Stitch	Chart pattern	Direction of knitting	Moss Stitch
	Braid pattern		

4 in. (10 cm)

Instead of buttons, you might choose a classic metal clasp or frog button closure—either would work well with this collar.

CHAPTER 2

Couture

MY WORK HAS ALWAYS BEEN FASHION-LED, WHETHER DOING design and production in the heady days of the '80s for Polo Ralph Lauren and other international fashion houses or creating my own ready-to-wear collections. However, for me, street fashion gives the biggest buzz. Bizarre combos that you couldn't create in your wildest dreams are often paraded casually on the sidewalks, and there's often a trickle-down effect to the catwalk.

Here you'll find easy-to-knit shawlettes with an eye toward avant-garde minimalism. If you're crazy for cables, try **Drift**, a chunky collar just oozing attitude. For maximum wow-factor there's **Enigma**, a diaphanous layered cape, and if you've never tried entrelac, **Harlequin** is sure to turn you on to this addictive technique. If you're looking for a relaxing weekend knit, both **Empty Circle** and **Twine** fit the bill. Black and white gives maximum impact to **Penumbra's** magical zigzag illusions.

The mood is cool and funky. Michael Nyman provides the soundtrack, with the spotlight on statement pieces that take you seamlessly through the day and into evening. Techniques showcased include cables, entrelac, and shadow knitting.

Drift Cowl

Don't be cowed by cables! This classy cowl is a great teacher and will have you cabling like a pro in no time—start it on a Friday evening and you'll wear it to work on Monday morning. With plenty of rest rows and virtually no finishing, you'll have spare time to find some fabulous buttons.

SKILL LEVEL
Easy

FINISHED MEASUREMENTS
8 in. (20 cm) wide, 28 in. (71 cm) long

YARN
Rowan Big Wool
87 yd. (80 m) per 100 g ball:
2 balls Vert 054

NOTIONS
1 pair size 17 U.S. (12 mm) needles
or size to obtain gauge
Cable needle
Size K-10½ U.S. (6.5 mm) crochet hook
Tapestry needle
3 buttons

GAUGE
13 sts and 13 rows = 4 in. (10 cm) in Cable Pattern

Note
For information on knitting cables, see p. 117.

Drift Schematic

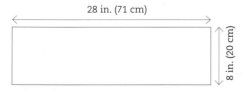

28 in. (71 cm)

8 in. (20 cm)

TO MAKE COWL
Cast on 26 sts and begin Cable Pattern (multiple of 12 sts).

Row 1 (Buttonhole row) Sl 1, k3, cast off 3 sts, k5, cast off 3 sts, k4, cast off 3 sts, k3, k1tbl.

Row 2 Sl 1, purl to last st, k1tbl, casting on over the cast-off sts as you come to them—26 sts.

Cont in Cable Pattern, beg on row 3 as follows (rows 1 and 2 have been worked already as buttonhole rows):

Row 1 Sl 1, knit to last st, k1tbl.

Row 2 Sl 1, purl to last st, k1tbl.

Row 3 Sl 1, *sl next 3 sts onto cn and hold at front of work, k3, k3 from cn, k6; rep from * to last st, k1tbl.

Row 4 Sl 1, purl to last st, k1tbl.

Row 5 Sl 1, knit to last st, k1tbl.

Row 6 Sl 1, purl to last st, k1tbl.

Row 7 Sl 1, *k6, sl next 3 sts to cn and hold at back of work, k3, k3 from cn; rep from * to last st, k1tbl.

Row 8 Sl 1, purl to last st, k1tbl.

Work all 8 rows of the Cable Pattern 11 times in all, then work rows 1–4 once—92 rows.

Work will measure approx 28 in. (71 cm) from the cast-on edge.

Cast off.

FINISHING
Work 1 row of single crochet (p. 120) at the cast-on and cast-off edges.

Securely weave in all ends.

Press lightly (p. 116) on the WS.

Neaten buttonholes and attach 3 buttons opposite the buttonholes along the cast-off edge.

Penumbra Cowl

Add a touch of magic to your knitting with this simple Japanese technique—shadow knitting. Alternate rows of light and shade, throw in a few sculptured stitches, and *presto*, an illusion occurs, tricking the eye into believing the colors are changing. I'm a big fan of pop art, and shadow knitting is a wonderful tool for creating bold optical knits. Wool/cotton yarn ensures fabulous stitch definition.

SKILL LEVEL
Intermediate

FINISHED MEASUREMENTS
12½ in. (31.7 cm) high, 25 in. (63.5 cm) around

YARN
Rowan Wool Cotton
123 yd. (113 m) per 50 g ball:
2 balls Inky 908 (A)
2 balls Antique 900 (B)

NOTIONS
Size 6 U.S. (4 mm) circular needle
or size to obtain gauge
Stitch marker
Tapestry needle

GAUGE
20 sts and 40 rows = 4 in. (10 cm) in Penumbra Chart pattern

TO MAKE COWL
Using yarn (A), cast on 124 sts and place marker. Join in the round, taking care not to twist the sts.
Work 6 rows of Garter St. in the round (p. 119), knitting and purling alternate rounds.
Attach yarn (B) and work the Penumbra Chart, rep the 31 sts 4 times on every round.
Work all 44 rounds twice, then work the first 22 rounds once.
Using yarn (A) only, work 6 rows in Garter St., knitting and purling alternate rounds.
Cast off as follows: K1, *pass this st back to the LH needle and k2tog; rep from * across row.

FINISHING
Using the tapestry needle, securely weave in ends.

continued on page 41

Penumbra Chart

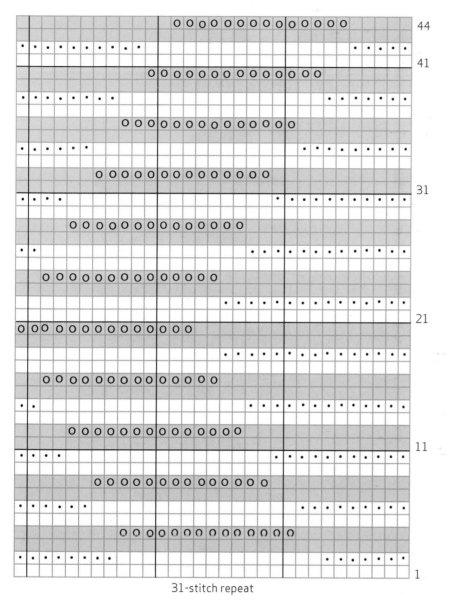

44

41

31

21

11

1

31-stitch repeat

The NB Chart is read from right to left on all rounds.

☐ K, using (B)

▧ K, using (A)

·̇ P, using (B)

Ⓞ P, using (A)

Penumbra Schematic

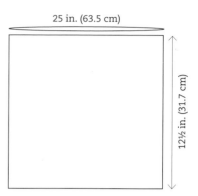

25 in. (63.5 cm)

12½ in. (31.7 cm)

At first glance, this appears to be a simple striped cowl. But look again and you'll see wide zigzags running top to bottom through the pattern.

Enigma Shawl

Strut your stuff in this dramatic and versatile two-piece shawl. The gossamer kidsilk drapes dreamily whether layered or worn separately. Wear it tied for a more structured look, or leave it to float free for a dramatic dose of mystery. Either way, you can be sure to make an entrance in this easy-to-knit shawl.

SKILL LEVEL
Easy

FINISHED MEASUREMENTS
Piece 1: 24 in. (61 cm) wide, 60 in. (152.5 cm) long
Piece 2: 34 in. (86 cm) long, 38 in. (96.5 cm) wide

YARN
Rowan Kidsilk Haze
229 yd. (210 m) per 25 g ball:
5 balls Jelly 597 (A)
3 balls Trance 582 (B)

NOTIONS
Size 5 U.S. (3.75 mm) circular needle
Size 7 U.S. (4.5 mm) circular needle
1 pair size 7 U.S. (4.5 mm) needles
or size to obtain gauge
Stitch marker
Tapestry needle

GAUGE
20 sts and 28 rows = 4 in. (10 cm) in Stockinette Stitch (p. 121)

Note
Slip the first stitch and knit into the back of the last stitch on every row.

TO MAKE SHAWL
Piece 1
Using size 7 U.S. (4.5 mm) needles and yarn (A), cast on 120 sts.
Work in Stockinette St. until the piece measures 25½ in. (65 cm), ending on a WS row.
Next row Work 60 sts, join a second ball of yarn, and work the rem 60 sts separately.
Cont in Stockinette St. until the piece measures 9 in. (23 cm) from beg of slit, ending on a WS row.
Cont as follows:
Next row Work across all sts.
Cont until the piece measures 60 in. (152.5 cm) from the cast-on edge, then cast off loosely.

Piece 2
Using size 7 U.S. (4.5 mm) needles and yarn (B), cast on 190 sts.
Work in Stockinette St. until the piece measures 12 in. (30.5 cm), ending on WS row.
Next row Work 95 sts, join a second ball of yarn, and work the rem 95 sts separately.
Cont in Stockinette St. until the piece measures 10 in. (25.5 cm) from beg of slit, ending on a WS row.
Cont as follows:
Next row Work across all sts.
Cont until the piece measures 34 in. (86 cm) from the cast-on edge, then cast off loosely.

continued on page 44

FINISHING

Piece 1

With RS facing so that the slit lies horizontally from right to left and determine where to pick up and knit the collar, 3 in. (7.5 cm) or one-third of the distance from the right edge of the neck edge. Using size 5 U.S. (3.75 mm) circular needle and (A), pick up and knit 34 sts to the beg of the slit, 50 sts across the back of the slit, and 16 sts across the front of the slit to the starting point—100 sts. Mark the first st. Working in the round, cont until the piece measures 6 in. (15 cm) from the picked up edge, ending on a WS row as follows:

Every round *K3, p2; rep from * around.

Then, change to the size 7 U.S. (4.5 mm) circular needle and work all rows back and forth in rib pattern as follows:

Row 1 *K3, p2; rep from * to end.
Row 2 *K2, p3; rep from * to end.
Rep these 2 rows until the piece measures a further 6 in. (15 cm) from the point at which the collar splits.
Cast off loosely in rib pattern using a larger needle, if necessary.

Piece 2

Using size 7 U.S. (4.5 mm) circular needle and (B), with RS facing, pick up and knit 50 sts along the front of the slit and 50 sts along the back—100 sts. Join in the round and cast off loosely.

Press both pieces lightly (p. 116) to size under a damp cloth, avoiding rib.

Enigma Schematic (Jelly)

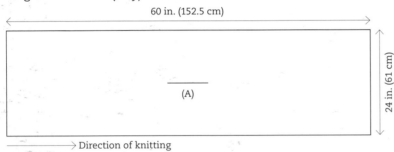

60 in. (152.5 cm)

(A)

24 in. (61 cm)

→ Direction of knitting

Enigma Schematic (Trance)

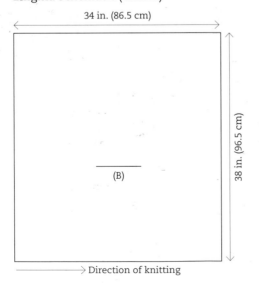

34 in. (86.5 cm)

(B)

38 in. (96.5 cm)

→ Direction of knitting

Two shawls in one, Enigma can be separated and worn as a single layer for a completely different warm-weather accessory.

Harlequin Cape

Hone your entrelac skills on this snug cape—which easily transforms into a collar. I chose Rowan's Colourscape yarn so that I could sit back and enjoy knitting the entrelac blocks knowing the colors would take care of themselves. Other handpaints should perform just as well, as long as you work a swatch first. You can then watch and wonder as you knit—the hues changing gradually before your eyes and fitting the blocks like magic!

SKILL LEVEL
Intermediate

FINISHED MEASUREMENTS
40 in. (101.6 cm) wide, 7 in. (18 cm) long

YARN
Rowan Colourscape Chunky
175 yd. (160 m) per 100 g skein:
2 skeins Carnival 430

NOTIONS
1 pair size 10½ U.S. (7 mm) needles
or size to obtain gauge
Size H-8 U.S. (5 mm) crochet hook
Large button

GAUGE
14 sts and 18 rows = 4 in. (10 cm) in
Stockinette Stitch (p. 121)

TO MAKE CAPE
Loosely cast on 88 sts and work in entrelac as follows:

Base triangles
First base triangle *P2, turn, k2, turn, p3, turn.
Cont in this way, purling 1 st more from the left needle each time, until there are 8 sts on the RH needle.
Do not turn.
Rep from * 10 times—11 base triangles.

First row of blocks
First edging triangle K2, turn, p2, turn, kfb, then skpo, turn, p3, turn, kfb, k1, then skpo, turn, p4, turn.
Cont in this way, dec 1 st from the base triangles on knit rows each time until kfb, k5, skpo has been worked.
Do not turn; leave these 8 sts.
Blocks *Pick up and knit 8 sts from the row ends of the first base triangle, turn, p8, turn, k7, skpo, turn, p8.
Cont in this way until all sts of the first base triangle have been decreased. Do not turn.
Rep from * for 9 more blocks across the row, picking up sts between the base triangles.
Second edging triangle Pick up and knit 8 sts from the row ends of the last base triangle, turn, p2tog, p6, turn, k7, turn. P2tog, p5, turn, k6.
Cont in this way, dec at the beg of every purl row until 1 st rem, turn, slip st onto the RH needle.

continued on page 48

Second row of blocks (no side triangles)

Blocks *P1, pick up and purl 7 sts, turn, k8, turn. P7, p2tog, turn, k8.

Cont in this way until all sts of the first row block have been decreased. Do not turn.

Work 10 more blocks in this way, picking up 8 sts.

Third row of blocks

Work as for the first row of blocks, working into the second row of blocks instead of into the base triangles.

Closing triangles

P1, *pick up and purl 7 sts from row-ends of the first side triangle, turn, k8, turn. P2tog, p5, p2tog, turn, k7, turn. P2tog, p4, p2tog, turn, k6, turn. Cont in this way until *turn, k2* has been worked, turn, p1, p2tog, turn, k2, turn, p3tog—1 st rem.

Rep from * to complete the other 10 closing triangles.

Fasten off rem st.

FINISHING

Securely weave in ends.

Press lightly (p. 116) on the WS.

Attach the button along the cast-on edge as desired. Using the crochet hook, make a single crochet chain (p. 120) about 4 in. (10 cm) long. Bend the chain into a loop and attach it to the side edge of the Cape at the apex of the first base triangle.

Harlequin Schematic

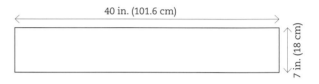

40 in. (101.6 cm)

7 in. (18 cm)

Whether neatly centered or worn to one side, a large, square button will highlight the woven-band effect of the entrelac technique.

Double-wrapped, the Harlequin Cape easily converts to a collar that will keep your neck warm and cozy on cold days.

Twine Cowl

This chunky cowl looks to the old craft of rope-making for its inspiration. Both abroad and closer to home, I've often watched fishermen on the quayside, mending nets, mooring their boats, raising sails— all activities dependent on rope. Traditionally, sailors have always sung shanties as they worked. Get in the groove with each of the three stitch patterns by creating a different song for each. Then you too can sing along as you knit!

SKILL LEVEL
Easy

FINISHED MEASUREMENTS
4 in. (10 cm) thick, approx 30 in. (76 cm) long

YARN
Rowan Big Wool
87 yd. (80 m) per 100 g ball:
2 balls each Linen 048 (A) and Eternal 055 (C)
1 ball Concrete 061 (B)

NOTIONS
1 pair size 17 U.S. (12 mm) needles *or size to obtain gauge,* plus 1 extra needle
Cable needle
3 stitch holders
Tapestry needle

GAUGE
9 sts and 12 rows = 4 in. (10 cm) in Stockinette Stitch (p. 121)

Note
Slip the first stitch and knit into the back of the last stitch on every row.

TO MAKE COWL
Work approx 34 in. (86 cm) each in the Cable, Moss St., and Rib patterns in the color as instructed, leaving sts on holders.

Cable Pattern (1)
Using yarn (B) cast on 12 sts.
Row 1 Sl 1, knit to last st, k1tbl.
Row 2 Sl 1, purl to last st, k1tbl.
Row 3 Sl 1, slip next 5 sts onto cn and hold at front of work, k5, k5 from cn, k1tbl.
Rows 4, 6, 8, and 10 Sl 1, purl to last st, k1tbl.
Rows 5, 7, and 9 Sl 1, knit to last st, k1tbl.
Rep these 10 rows until the piece measures approx 34 in. (86 cm), ending on row 6. Place sts on holder.

Moss Stitch Pattern (2)
Using yarn (A), cast on 15 sts.
Row 1 Sl 1, *k1, p1; rep from * to last 2 sts, k1, k1tbl.
Rep row 1 to end. Place sts on holder.

continued on page 50

Rib Pattern (3)
Using yarn (C), cast on 14 sts.
Row 1 Sl 1, *k2, p2; rep from * to last st, k1tbl.
Rep this row to end. Place sts on holder.

FINISHING
Using size 17 U.S. (12 mm) needles, place 15 sts of
Moss St. pattern on a needle, then 12 sts of Cable
pattern, and then 14 sts of Rib pattern—41 sts.
With RS facing, bring strand (C) over (B) and
(A), finishing on the left of the pieces, then do
the same in turn with strand (B) and strand (A),
continuing until the Cowl is completely twisted,
ending with yarn (C) on the RH side of the piece,
as at top.
With RS facing, pick up and knit 41 sts across
the bottom of the piece in the same order as the
stitches on the needle at the top.
With RS together, work a Three-Needle Bind-Off
(p. 121) using the extra needle, keeping colors
correct.

Fold patterns 1 and 3 in half and arrange the cables
to sit on the outside of the work. For extra stability,
add sts here and there in the appropriate color
yarn to secure.
Securely weave in ends.

Twine Schematic

Twist the three ends together.

30 in. (76 cm) finished
34 in. (86.5 cm) before twisting

| Moss St. Pattern 2 in (A) | Cable Pattern 1 in (B) | Rib Pattern 3 in (C) |

Twist patterns 3, 1, and 2
(respectively) over to the left
until entire cowl is twisted,
ending in the same position
as shown.

*It's all in the twist: The secret to Twine's wonderful,
woven-rope look is the final step, which makes a rectangle
into a twisting Möbius strip of alternating textures.*

Empty Circle Joined Hat and Scarf

An ancient and universal symbol of unity and infinity, the empty circle is a fascinating concept of balance, one that denotes both fullness and emptiness. This quick moss stitch project is knit in lofty merino, and the circles are created merely by casting on and off on successive rows. In the spirit of yin and yang, this chic hat and scarf combo will keep you toasty warm whilst looking ultra cool.

SKILL LEVEL
Easy

FINISHED MEASUREMENTS
Hat: 20 in. (51 cm) around
Scarf flaps: 5 in. (12.7 cm) wide, 32 in. (81 cm) long (x2)

YARN
Rowan Drift
87 yd. (80 m) per 100 g ball:
2 balls Fire 906 (A)
1 ball Nomad 907 (B)

NOTIONS
1 pair size 13 U.S. (9 mm) needles
1 pair size 15 U.S. (10 mm) needles
or size to obtain gauge
Size K-10½ U.S. (6.5 mm) crochet hook
Stitch holders
Tapestry needle
Polyester fiberfill

GAUGE
10 sts and 18 rows = 4 in. (10 cm) in Moss Stitch (p. 119)

Note
Slip the first stitch and knit into the back of the last stitch on every row.

TO MAKE SCARF AND HAT
Scarf (Make 2)
Using size 15 U.S. (10 mm) needles, cast on 13 sts in yarn (A) and cont in Moss St. to end. When the work measures 4 in. (10 cm) from the cast-on edge, ending on a WS row, work the Circle Rows as follows:

Next row Work 3 sts in Moss St., cast off 7 sts, work 3 sts in Moss St.

Next row Work 3 sts in Moss St., cast on 7 sts using the Backward Loop Cast-On (p. 116), work 3 sts in Moss St. *Work a further 4 in. (10 cm) in Moss St., then work the 2 Circle Rows as set**.

Rep from * to ** twice more, then work a further 4 in. (10 cm) in Moss St.

Break the yarn and leave the sts on holders.

Hat
Using size 13 U.S. (9 mm) needles, cast on 4 sts in yarn (B).

With RS facing, knit 13 sts from a holder, and cast on 16 sts. With RS still facing, knit 13 sts from the other holder, and cast on a further 4 sts—50 sts.

Work in Moss St. for 3 rows, then cont as follows:

Next row (RS) *Work 2 sts in Moss St., cast off 5 sts in Moss St., work 3 sts in Moss St.; rep from * to end.

Next row *Work 3 sts in Moss St., cast on 5 sts using the Backward Loop Cast-On, work 2 sts in Moss St.; rep from * to end.

Work 2 more rows in Moss St.

continued on page 54

Change to larger needles and knit 1 row. Change to yarn (A) and cont in Stockinette St. to end (p. 121). Work as set until the work measures 6 in. (15 cm) from the cast-on edge, ending on a WS row.

Shape crown

Row 1 (RS) *K5, k2tog; rep from * to last st, k1—43 sts.
Row 2 Purl.
Row 3 *K4, k2tog; rep from * to last st, k1—36 sts.
Row 4 Purl.
Row 5 *K3, k2tog; rep from * to last st, k1—29 sts.
Row 6 Purl.
Row 7 *K2, k2tog; rep from * to last st, k1—22 sts.
Break off yarn and, using the tapestry needle, thread it through the remaining sts, pull tight, and secure firmly on the inside of the Hat.

FINISHING

Oversew the back seam of Hat on the inside. Using yarn (B), work 1 round of single crochet (p. 120) around each hole on the Scarf and secure the yarn by weaving the ends into the appropriate color. Using yarn (A), work 1 round of single crochet around each hole on the Hat and secure the yarn in the same way.

Ball (Make 2)

Using size 15 U.S. (10 mm) needles, cast on 8 sts in yarn (B), leaving a long tail for sewing.
Row 1 Knit into the front and back of every st—16 sts.
Row 2 (and all even-numbered rows) Purl.
Row 3 (and all odd-numbered rows) Knit.
Row 11 *K2tog; rep from * to end—8 sts.
With the tapestry needle, run yarn through all 8 sts and gather, securing the tail. Using the tapestry needle and cast-on tail, thread through the cast-on sts and gather, securing the tail. Stuff with polyester fiberfill.
Using the tapestry needle, sew the side edges together.
Attach one ball to one end of each Scarf piece, gathering the edges before attaching the balls. Thread the tapestry needle with yarn (B).
Go through the base of each ball to the top so that the tail is lost, then wrap the yarn several times around the point where the end of the Scarf and the top of the ball meet, to neaten the join. Fasten off, then take the needle back into each ball to secure the tail.

Empty Circle Schematic

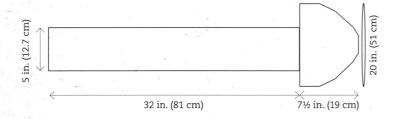

5 in. (12.7 cm)

20 in. (51 cm)

32 in. (81 cm) 7½ in. (19 cm)

Endlessly stylish but easy to make, this scarf and hat combo knits up fast in chunky merino and can easily be finished in a weekend.

CHAPTER 3

Folk

MY GRANDMOTHER TAUGHT ME TO KNIT AS SOON AS I COULD
hold the needles, so it's always been a part of my life. I love to contemplate an
old piece of knitting, curious about the person who created it. I imagine the
radio's playing bluegrass and the time is twilight, the moment between light
and dark, the link between past and present.

Here time-honored textiles such as Scottish Fair Isles and tartans, Irish
arans, fisher ganseys, and patchwork inform my contemporary designs.
Although knit in lace, **Arabesque** is a true Möbius scarf, and denim yarn
breathes new life into the gansey stitches of **Polperro**. Brush up your Fair
Isle skills with **Bess's** bicolored rib, whilst for the more experienced there's
Miss Garricks, finished with recycled crystal beads. For fans of modular knits,
there's **Purple Patch**, and if intarsia lights your fire, **Ceilidh** is a plaid with no
shortage of oomph factor.

I hope these new ways with traditional techniques will inspire you. Four
pillars of traditional knitting are showcased: two-color stranded knitting, intarsia, cables, and lace. Edgings include single crochet and picot point cast-off.

Miss Garricks Cowl

The two Miss Garricks are a pair of sisters from Shetland, Scotland. I never fail to be inspired by the ladies' intricate Fair Isles, so this design is for them, evoking the misty, moisty mornings of their island home. I added the vintage crystal beads to reflect color just like dewdrops. Though not a Fair Isle for the faint-hearted, the pattern is knit traditionally in the round so you can see the pattern develop and spot any mistakes as they happen.

SKILL LEVEL
Experienced

FINISHED MEASUREMENTS
16 in. (40.5 cm) high,
28 in. (71 cm) around

YARN
Rowan Cocoon
126 yd. (115 m) per 100 g ball:
1 ball each Bilberry 812 (A), Petal 823 (B),
Kiwi 816 (C), Seascape 813 (D), Frost 806
(E), Quarry Tile 818 (F), Misty Blue 827
(G), and Tundra 808 (H)

NOTIONS
Size 10½ U.S. (7 mm) circular needle
or size to obtain gauge
Size J-10 U.S. (6 mm) crochet hook
Stitch markers
Tapestry needle
10 crystal beads

GAUGE
16 sts and 15 rows = 4 in. (10 cm)
in Miss Garricks Chart pattern

TO MAKE COWL
Using yarn (A), cast on 112 sts and place marker.
Join in the round, taking care not to twist the sts.
Work all 16 sts of the Miss Garricks Chart seven times around.
Work the 56 rounds and cast off in yarn (A).

FINISHING
Using the tapestry needle, securely weave in ends.
Press lightly (p. 116) on the WS.
Using the crochet hook and yarn (F), make a single crochet chain (p. 120) about 42 in. (106.5 cm) long. Thread the crochet chain through the yarn-over sts (row 49) at the top of the cowl. Attach 5 beads to each end of the crochet chain.
Work 3 rounds of single crochet at the cast-on and cast-off edges of the cowl, alternating rounds in yarns (F), (E), and (F).

continued on page 61

Tiny crystal beads add sparkle and make the perfect finishing touch for the cowl's ties.

Miss Garricks Chart

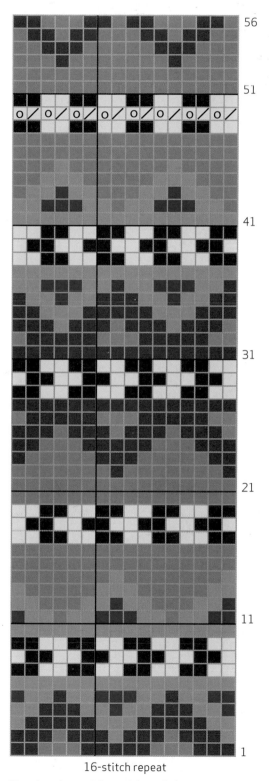

- ■ A Bilberry 812
- ■ B Petal 823
- ■ C Kiwi 816
- ■ D Seascape 813
- ☐ E Frost 806
- ⊙ Yo, using (E)
- ╱ K2tog, using (E)
- ■ F Quarry Tile 818
- ■ G Misty Blue 827
- ■ H Tundra 808

16-stitch repeat

The chart is read from right to left on all rows.

Miss Garricks Schematic

28 in. (71 cm)

16 in. (40.5 cm)

Arabesque Scarf

I find myself revisiting this traditional and versatile lace pattern over and over again, as it reminds me of my English Lancashire childhood. My mother loved this pattern—easy to knit, but creating a deceptively intricate design. Here I've chosen a reversible garter stitch version, so that this true Möbius scarf will look great on both sides, and a gorgeous cashmerino and silk fiber to guarantee stitch definition.

SKILL LEVEL
Intermediate

FINISHED MEASUREMENTS
Small: 36 in. (91.4 cm) around,
3½ in. (9 cm) high
Large: 50 in. (127 cm) around,
7½ in. (19 cm) high
*Pattern is written for size Small,
with Large instructions in
parentheses where necessary.*

YARN
Sublime Cashmere Merino Silk Aran
94 yd. (86 m) per 50 g ball:
2 balls Rhubarb 107 (Small)
5 balls Artichoke 108 (Large)

NOTIONS
Size 8 U.S. (5 mm) extra-long circular
needle *or size to obtain gauge*
Stitch markers
Tapestry needle

GAUGE
20 sts and 30 rows = 4 in. (10 cm)
in Feather and Fan pattern

TO MAKE SCARF
Loosely cast on 180 (252) sts and begin Feather and Fan pattern (multiple of 12 sts).
Round 1 Ensuring sts are not twisted, pick up and knit 1 st in the thread below the first cast-on st, along the lower edge of the cast-on row. Leave the first cast-on st on the needle. This closes the circle. Cont around in this way, picking up 1 st below each of the original cast-on sts and leaving all the cast-on sts on their needle—360 (504) sts.
Round 2 Place marker on the RH needle. Make sure the work is not twisted, then purl around back to marker.
Round 3 *(K2tog) twice, (yo, k1) 4 times, (k2tog) twice; rep from * around.
Round 4 Purl.
Round 5 Knit.
Cont in feather and fan pattern, repeating rounds 2–5 until the work measures approx 3 in. (7.5 cm) [7 in. (18 cm)], ending on round 4.
Cast off using the picot point cast-off: Cast off 2 sts, *sl rem st on RH needle onto the LH needle, cast on 2 sts, cast off 4 sts; rep from * to end and fasten off rem st.

FINISHING
Securely weave in ends. Press lightly (p. 116) on the WS to size.

continued on page 65

Arabesque Schematic

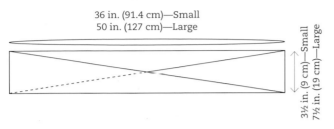

36 in. (91.4 cm)—Small
50 in. (127 cm)—Large

3½ in. (9 cm)—Small
7½ in. (19 cm)—Large

At just over 4 feet, Arabesque can be worn long and loose (above), wrapped and pinned (p. 62), or knit in a smaller size (opposite) for a sweet double necklet.

The feather and fan stitch pattern is a traditional favorite that reverses and looks beautiful on either side.

Bess Ruff

The exquisite Tudor neck ruffs worn by Good Queen Bess inspired this striking design. The corrugated rib will get you up to speed for future Fair Isle projects, whilst the simple frill would add a touch of glamour to any scarf. Stylish and cozy, it stows away neatly in your purse—I won't be leaving home without mine this winter!

SKILL LEVEL
Intermediate

FINISHED MEASUREMENTS
16 in. (40.5 cm) wide, 5½ in. (14 cm) high

YARN
Rowan Silk Twist
93 yd. (85 m) per 50 g ball:
1 ball Ebony 671 (A)
1 ball Ruby 668 (B)

NOTIONS
1 pair size 6 U.S. (4 mm) needles
1 pair size 8 U.S. (5 mm) needles
or size to obtain gauge
Stitch markers
Tapestry needle
5 buttons

GAUGE
20 sts and 22 rows = 4 in. (10 cm) in Corrugated Rib

Notes
Slip the first stitch and knit into the back of the last stitch on every row. For information on knitting Fair Isle, see p. 118.

TO MAKE RUFF
Using size 8 U.S. (5 mm) needles and yarn (A), cast on 78 sts and work in Corrugated Rib as follows:
Row 1 (RS) *K2 in (B), p2 in (A), rep from * to last 2 sts, k2 in (B).
Row 2 *P2 in (B), k2 in (A), rep from * to last 2 sts, p2 in (B).
Work as set until the piece measures 5 in. (12.75 cm), ending on a WS row.
Change to size 6 U.S. (4 mm) needles and yarn (A), cont in Stockinette St. to end:
Next row (RS) Knit into the front and back of every st—156 sts.
Next row Purl into the back and front of every st—312 sts.
Cast off using the picot point cast-off: Cast off 2 sts, *sl rem st on RH needle onto LH needle, cast on 1 st, cast off 3 sts; rep from * to end and fasten off rem st.

FINISHING
Button Band
Using size 6 U.S. (4 mm) needles and yarn (A), with RS facing, pick up and knit 23 sts along the top left side edge, below the frill, to the bottom of the side edge.
Work 5 rows in Moss St. as follows:
Row 1 *K1, p1; rep from * to end.
Row 2 Purl the knit sts and knit the purl sts.
Rep row 2 three more times.
Cast off in Moss St.

continued on page 69

Details such as lace edging and neat rows of little round buttons were hallmarks of Elizabethan dress, and give Bess old-fashioned charm.

Buttonhole Band

Work in the same way as button band,
inserting 5 buttonholes on row 3 as follows:
Mark the position of the 5 buttons on the button
band so that the 1st and 5th buttons are marked
2 sts from each edge and the other 3 buttons
are spaced evenly between.
Cast off 2 sts at each marker, casting them
on again on the following row.
Attach the buttons opposite the buttonholes.
To encourage the frill to stand up, thread the
tapestry needle with yarn (A) and sew a small
running st around the 1st row of frill. Pull the yarn
tight until the frill fits the top of the Ruff, then
securely fasten off.

Bess Schematic

16 in. (40.5 cm)

5½ in. (14 cm)

The Elizabethan Ruff

Queen Elizabeth I was a dedicated
follower of fashion and dressed to
impress. Clothes were an important
status symbol for the Elizabethans,
so the queen's attire had to be mag-
nificent to outshine her courtiers.
Neck ruffs, the intricate collars worn
by both men and women of the time,
became more and more elaborate as
markers of social standing. These
must-have pieces, kept in place using
elaborate supports and underprops,
framed the face and dictated the hair-
styles of the period. Women's ruffs
acquired a more feminine and seduc-
tive style by opening at the front to
expose cleavage. With the introduc-
tion of starch in 1564, ruffs became
ever more extravagant, and women's
ruffs often were further decorated
with lace, gold and silver threads, and
fine silk. They sparkled with images of
the sun, moon, and stars. The hugely
expensive handmade lace or frilled
fine linen needed to make a ruff
ensured that only the wealthy could
afford such an exquisite accessory.

Ceilidh Shawlette

I love to dance and I've always adored tartans—and this shawlette is inspired by both, taking its name from the Gaelic word for *party*. As a child growing up in a Lancashire mill town, I wore a kilt every winter—a bold splash of color during those cold, gray days. There's something joyous about the way a kilt swings, giving the wearer built-in sashay. If you're lucky enough to have your own clan plaid, just recolor the chart to match. The tweedy and sumptuous alpaca yarn is light yet warm, making this shawlette the perfect piece to wear to the next ceilidh!

SKILL LEVEL
Experienced

FINISHED MEASUREMENTS
26 in. (66 cm) wide at shoulder, 10 in. (25.5 cm) long without collar

YARN
Rowan Lima
109 yd. (100 m) per 50 g ball:
4 balls Machu Picchu 885 (A)
1 ball each Titicaca 883 (B), Guatemala 892 (C), La Paz 891 (D), Puno 886 (F), and Nazca 887 (G)
2 balls Chile 882 (E)

NOTIONS
1 pair size 9 U.S. (5.5 mm) needles
or size to obtain gauge
Size 7 U.S. (4.5 mm) circular needle
Size 8 U.S. (5 mm) circular needle
Size G-6 U.S. (4 mm) crochet hook
Stitch markers
Tapestry needle

GAUGE
20 sts and 26 rows = 4 in. (10 cm) in Ceilidh Chart pattern

Note
For information on knitting intarsia, see p. 119.

TO MAKE SHAWLETTE
Using size 9 U.S. (5.5 mm) needles and yarn (A), cast on 51 sts.
Work all 30 rows of the Ceilidh Chart, centering the chart as follows:
RS rows Work the last 5 sts of the chart, work all 20 sts twice, work the first 6 sts.
WS rows Work the last 6 sts of the chart, work all 20 sts twice, work the first 5 sts.
Cont in this way until the piece measures 46 in. (117 cm).
Cast off.

FINISHING
Place markers 10 in. (25.5 cm) from the cast-on and cast-off edges along top side edge.
Position the shawl's cast-off edge on a flat surface in front of you. Arrange the shawl's length counter-clockwise, so that the cast-on edge completely overlaps the cast-off edge, ending along its side edge, forming a

continued on page 72

Ceilidh Chart

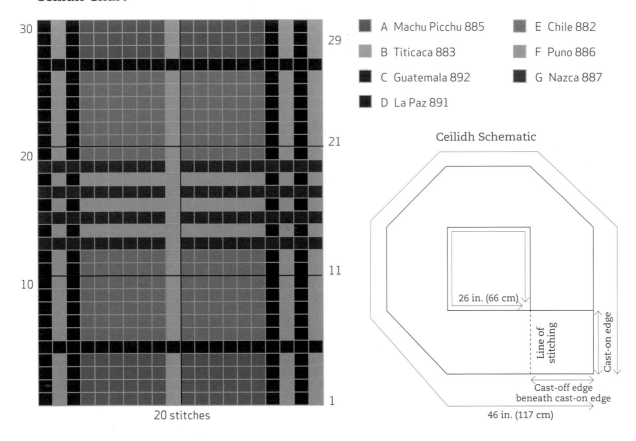

30 / 29 / 21 / 20 / 11 / 10 / 1

20 stitches

A Machu Picchu 885
B Titicaca 883
C Guatemala 892
D La Paz 891
E Chile 882
F Puno 886
G Nazca 887

Ceilidh Schematic

26 in. (66 cm)
Line of stitching
Cast-on edge
Cast-off edge beneath cast-on edge
46 in. (117 cm)

---

circle shape, as indicated on the schematic (above). Using the tapestry needle, slip stitch along the inside edge where the two ends overlap to join the ends into a circle.

Collar

Using size 7 U.S. (4.5 mm) circular needle and yarn (A), pick up and knit 150 sts around the inner neckline, beginning at the center back with RS facing.

Round 1 *K1, p1; rep from * around.

Rep this round until the collar measures 6½ in. (16.5 cm).

Change to size 8 U.S. (5 mm) circular needle and cont as set until the collar measures 13¾ in. (35 cm), then change to yarn (E) and work 1 row. Loosely cast off in rib.

Using yarn (A), with RS facing, work 1 row of single crochet (p. 120) as follows:

1. Through two thicknesses of cast-on edge and last 10 in. (25.5 cm) of shawl.
2. Through two thicknesses along cast-off edge and first 10 in. (25.5 cm) of shawl.
3. Through one thickness around inside edge of shawl.
4. Through one thickness from start of cast-on edge along side edge for 6 in. (15.2 cm) then through two thicknesses over remaining 4 in. (10 cm).

Using the tapestry needle, weave the ends into like colors. Press lightly (p. 116) on the WS, avoiding the ribbing.

On the final crocheted
seam from side edge to
neck, leave the first 6 in.
(15 cm) open so that the
end hangs down. Hold
this flap in place with
a traditional kilt pin—
choices range from the
very basic to ornate family
crests and Celtic symbols.

Purple Patch Shrug

Don't you just love patchwork, as old as time and especially popular in difficult periods when folk just have to make do? I've used super-soft fingering weight yarn, but this is also a good stash-busting project. It's an easy garter stitch knit, so you can let your imagination run riot with the embellishments. Raid the thrift stores for vintage buttons and beads, add feathers or tiny bells to adorn the edges, or, like me, use buttons to evoke the Cockney spirit of London's Pearly Kings and Queens.

SKILL LEVEL
Easy

FINISHED MEASUREMENTS
27 in. (68.5 cm) wide, 15 in. (38 cm) long excluding crochet

YARN
Rowan Milk Cotton Fine
164 yd. (150 m) per 50 g ball:
1 ball Ardour 508 (A), Scented Satin 488 (B), Water Bomb 498 (C), Sepia 501 (D), Shrimps 483 (E), Opaque 506 (F)

NOTIONS
1 pair size 2 U.S. (2.75 mm) needles *or size to obtain gauge*
Size D-3 U.S. (3.25 mm) crochet hook
Tapestry needle
Stitch markers
44 pearl buttons, 3/8 in. (12 mm) in diameter

GAUGE
28 sts and 48 rows = 4 in. (10 cm)
in Garter Stitch (p. 119)

Note
Slip the first stitch and knit into the back of the last stitch on every row.

TO MAKE SHRUG
Squares
Cast on 20 sts and work 36 rows in Garter St.
Cast off.
Work 8 squares in Garter St. using yarn (B).
Work 9 squares in Garter St. using yarn (C).
Work 7 squares in Garter St. using yarn (D).
Work 5 squares in Garter St. using yarn (E).
Work 4 squares in Garter St. using yarn (F).

FINISHING
Using the tapestry needle, securely weave in ends. Following the color arrangement and direction of knitting indicated on the schematic, crochet together the Garter St. squares using yarn (A) as follows:
Place two squares together with WS facing each other. With RS facing you, join the yarn with a slip st in the back loop of the cast-on/cast-off edges (or thread between the notches on the side edges) of the front square.
*Ch 1 working in the back loop of the square in front and in the front loop of the square in back (or thread between the notches on the side edges). Ch 1 through both loops. Rep from *.

continued on page 76

Purple Patch Schematic

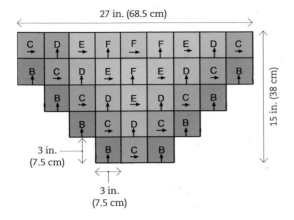

27 in. (68.5 cm)

C	D	E	F	F	F	E	D	C
B	C	D	E	F	E	D	C	B
	B	C	D	E	D	C	B	
		B	C	D	C	B		
			B	C	B			

15 in. (38 cm)

3 in. (7.5 cm)

3 in. (7.5 cm)

↑ Direction of knitting, bottom to top

→ Direction of knitting, left to right

Note: Measurements do not include the crochet join.

Piece together the squares into lengthwise rows, then join together the rows. Cont until all squares and joined pieces are attached, as indicated on the schematic.

Note: In my design, each square is placed at a right angle to the previous color, creating a textured checkerboard effect.

Border

Starting at the top right corner of the Shrug (square C), work 1 round of single crochet (p. 120) around the perimeter of shawl using yarn (A).

Work a second round single crochet, inserting buttonholes as follows:

Mark the position of 6 buttonholes evenly spaced on the top right edge, 3 each on squares D and C. Crochet to marker, *ch3, skip 1 st, sl 1 into next st, cont to next marker and rep from * until 6 buttonholes are worked.

Work a third round of single crochet and fasten off. Attach 6 buttons on the top left edge, 3 each on squares D and C, opposite the buttonholes worked on the top right edge.

Attach 1 button on each corner of every square, excluding the top edge—38 buttons attached.

Pearl buttons are actually made from shell, and the real article is not as common as synthetic copies. Their delicate beauty is worth scavenging for, however. Try vintage stores and flea markets.

Polperro Cape

The pretty Cornish village of Polperro, with its long knitting tradition, must have spawned many a gansey pattern. I like to imagine that the knitters there would appreciate this new take on their patterns. The denim yarn is hard wearing and gives great stitch definition as the color of the raised stitches starts to fade after a few washes. My wooden buckle complements the workwear look, but if you feel a Western moment coming on, a silver and turquoise buckle would add instant Navajo style.

SKILL LEVEL
Intermediate

FINISHED MEASUREMENTS
Approx 32 in. (81.5 cm) wide at shoulder, 14 in. (35.5 cm) long after washing

YARN
Rowan Denim
109 yd. (100 m) per 50 g ball:
6 balls Memphis 229
Yarn shrinks approx one-eighth in length when washed.

NOTIONS
1 pair size 3 U.S. (3.25 mm) needles
1 pair size 6 U.S. (4 mm) needles
or size to obtain gauge
Stitch markers
Tapestry needle
Buckle

GAUGE
24 sts and 32 rows = 4 in. (10 cm) in Polperro Chart pattern

TO MAKE CAPE
Using size 3 U.S. (3.25 mm) needles, cast on 70 sts and work 6 rows of Garter St. (p. 119).
Change to size 6 U.S. (4 mm) needles and begin working the Polperro Chart. Rep all 8 rows until the work measures approx 43 in. (109 cm) from the cast-on edge, ending on row 8.
Change to the smaller needles and work 6 rows in Garter St.
Cast off loosely.

Band
Using the smaller needles, cast on 25 sts and work as follows:
RS rows K12, p1, work sts 30–41 of the chart.
WS rows Work sts 30–41 of the chart, p13.
Keep cables, Stockinette St. (p. 121), and fold line sts correct as you knit.
Cont as set until the Band measures 41 in. (104 cm) from the cast-on edge, ending on either row 4 or row 8 of the chart pattern.
Cast off.

continued on page 81

*For an equally stunning
wrap, choose cashmerino DK,
work an extra 12 in. (30 cm)
of the cable pattern, and
omit the collar.*

FINISHING

Sew a running stitch along the top edge of the Cape, gather until the edge measures 36 in. (91.5 cm), and secure.

Fold the Band in two along the fold line and slip-stitch cables to the facing at the cast-on and cast-off edges.

Starting at the left front edge, with the RS of the Cape facing the cabled edge of the Band, sew the Band to the Cape, leaving an extra 5 in. (12.7 cm) unsewn at the right front edge to go through the buckle.

To achieve given measurements, machine-wash the Cape in warm water, about 60°F (15.5°C), spin well, and tumble dry. Always wash the finished Cape separately.

Attach the buckle to the band at the left front edge.

Polperro Chart

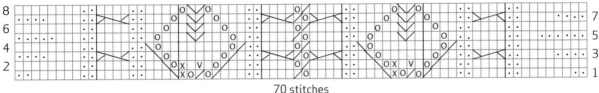

70 stitches

☐	K on RS, p on WS
·	P on RS, k on WS
⟋	K2tog on RS, p2tog on WS
O	Yo
X	No stitch
⟍	Ssk on RS, p2tog-b on WS
V	Inc 1—p1, p1-b in 1 st
⟍⟋	Sl 2 sts on cn and hold at back, k2, k2 from cn.
⟋⟍	Sl 2 sts on cn and hold at front, k2, k2 from cn.

Polperro Schematic

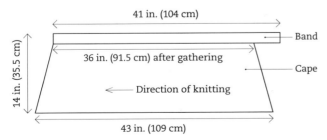

41 in. (104 cm)

— Band

36 in. (91.5 cm) after gathering

— Cape

⟵ Direction of knitting

14 in. (35.5 cm)

43 in. (109 cm)

Note: Measurements before washing

CHAPTER 4

Vintage

LOOKING TO FASHION THROUGH THE AGES FOR THEIR DESIGN sensibility, these jabots, frills, mantillas, and capes take us on a brief journey through costume history.

Taking ideas from the Tudors through to the screen icons of the 1950s, here I've tried to recapture some vintage magic. For beginners there's **Vamp**—a boa in mohair and kid silk. **Grace** features a simple dropped-stitch pattern and can be worn two ways for maximum versatility. Entrelac is featured once more in **Treasure**—an exquisite silk jabot. The intricate **Mantilla** will appeal to lace fanatics, and for lovers of top-down lace shawls, there's **Brontë**. Intarsia knitters will find the leopard-print **Kitty** ready for as much glam as they can give it, and for fans of beading and short-row techniques, there's **Fizz**, a sophisticated capelet inspired by Audrey Hepburn.

So put bebop on the hi-fi, crack open the bubbly, then sit back and sparkle with old-style glamour when you wear your new vintage shawlette. Techniques showcased are intarsia, lace, entrelac, beaded knitting, and dropped stitchwork. Edgings include shell crochet, I-cord, picot point cast-off, and frills.

Kitty Capelet

Leopard prints have been de rigueur for any self-respecting glamour-puss since Hollywood started making films. From the quintessential 1950s pinup Bettie Page in *The Girl in the Leopard Print Bikini* to soap opera sirens like Bet Lynch in the mother of all British soaps *Coronation Street*, the leopard print is synonymous with sexy. Even Bob Dylan referenced it in his song "Leopard-Skin Pill-Box Hat" from the *Blonde on Blonde* album. My little leopard-print number is knit intarsia—a racy little capelet to bring out the animal in you.

SKILL LEVEL
Experienced

FINISHED MEASUREMENTS
Small: To fit bust 30–32 in. (76–81 cm);
8 in. (20 cm) wide at neck edge,
12 in. (30.5 cm) long
Medium: To fit bust 34–36 in. (86–91 cm);
8½ in. (21.5 cm) wide at neck edge,
12½ in. (31.7 cm) long
Large: To fit bust 38–40 in. (96–101 cm);
8¾ in. (22.3 cm) at neck edge,
13 in. (33 cm) long
Pattern is written for size Small, with Medium and Large instructions in parentheses where necessary.

YARN
Rowan Felted Tweed DK
191 yd. (175 m) per 50 g ball:
3 (3, 4) balls Gilt 160 (A)
1 (2, 2) balls Cinnamon 175 (B)
1 (2, 2) balls Ginger 154 (C)

NOTIONS
1 pair size 3 U.S. (3.25 mm) straight needles or extra-long circular needle
1 pair size 6 U.S. (4 mm) straight needles or extra-long circular needle *or size to obtain gauge*
Stitch holders
4 buttons

GAUGE
28 sts and 28 rows = 4 in. (10 cm) in Kitty Chart pattern

Note
For information on knitting intarsia, see p. 119.

TO MAKE CAPELET
Using size 3 U.S. (3.25 mm) needles and yarn (A), cast on 294 (336, 378) sts.
Work in Stockinette St. (p. 121) back and forth until the piece measures 1 in. (2.5 cm) from the cast-on edge, ending with a RS row. Knit 1 row to form fold line.
Work a further 1 in. (2.5 cm) in Moss St. (p. 119).
Change to size 6 U.S. (4 mm) needles and work the Kitty Chart, centering pattern as follows:
Work the last 3 (0, 21) sts of the chart, work the 48 sts 6 (7, 7) times, work the first 3 (0, 21) sts. When the work measures 7 (7½, 8) in. [18 (19, 20) cm] from the fold line, end the pattern on a WS row.

continued on page 86

Kitty Chart

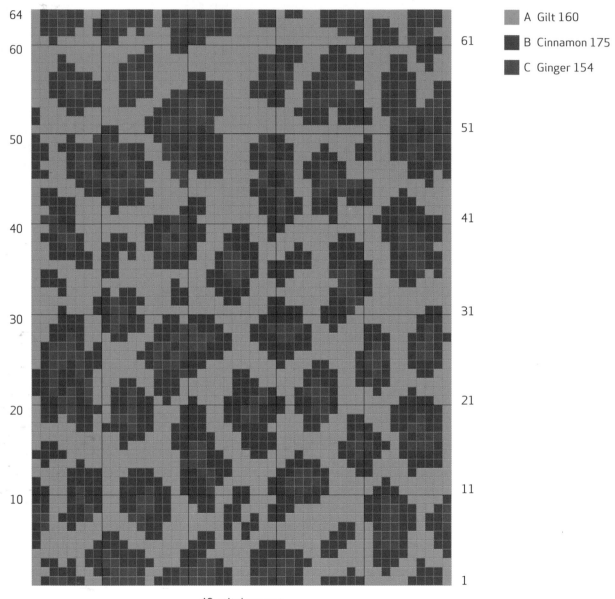

64
60
50
40
30
20
10

61
51
41
31
21
11
1

continued on page 88

48-stitch repeat

A Gilt 160
B Cinnamon 175
C Ginger 154

Kitty Schematic

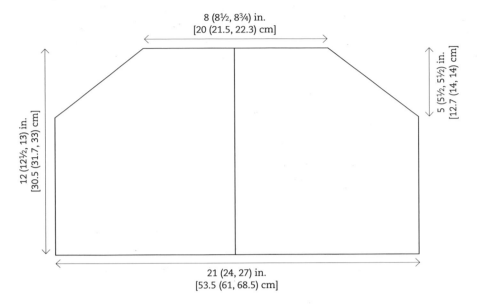

8 (8½, 8¾) in.
[20 (21.5, 22.3) cm]

5 (5½, 5½) in.
[12.7 (14, 14) cm]

12 (12½, 13) in.
[30.5 (31.7, 33) cm]

21 (24, 27) in.
[53.5 (61, 68.5) cm]

Shape Top of Capelet

Note: Work these 6 rows as instructed for the appropriate size.

Next row (RS) Keeping pattern correct as set, work 47 (54, 59) sts, k3tog, work 46 (54, 64) sts, k3tog tbl, work 96 (108, 120) sts, k3tog, work 46 (54, 64) sts, k3tog tbl, work 47 (54, 59) sts—286 (328, 370) sts.

Next row (WS) Keeping pattern correct as set, work 46 (53, 58) sts, p3tog tbl, work 44 (52, 62) sts, p3tog, work 94 (106, 118) sts, p3tog tbl, work 44 (52, 62) sts, p3tog, work 46 (53, 58) sts—278 (320, 362) sts.

Next row (RS) Work as set with no dec.

Next row (WS) Keeping pattern correct as set, work 45 (52, 57) sts, p3tog tbl, work 42 (50, 60) sts, p3tog, work 92 (104, 116) sts, p3tog tbl, work 42 (50, 60) sts, p3tog, work 45 (52, 57) sts—270 (312, 354) sts.

Next row (RS) Keeping pattern correct as set, work 44 (51, 56) sts, k3tog, work 40 (48, 58) sts, k3tog tbl, work 90 (102, 114) sts, k3tog, work 40 (48, 58) sts, k3tog tbl, work 44 (51, 56) sts—262 (304, 346) sts.

Next row (WS) Work as set with no dec.

For Small size

Work these 6 rows 5 times, dec as set, then work rows 1–4 so that final row should read: Keeping pattern correct as set, work 25 sts, p3tog tbl, work 2, p3tog, work 52 sts, p3tog tbl, work 2, p3tog, work 25 sts—110 sts.

Work 2 rows in pattern as set. Cast off.

For Medium size

Work these 6 rows 5 times, then dec every row 7 times so that final row should read: Keeping pattern correct as set, work 28 sts, k3tog, work 2, k3tog tbl, work 56 sts, k3tog, work 2, k3tog tbl, work 28 sts—120 sts.

Work 1 row in pattern as set. Cast off.

For Large size

Work these 6 rows twice, then dec every row 24 times so that final row should read: Keeping pattern correct as set, work 28 sts, p3tog tbl, work 2, p3tog, work 58 sts, p3tog tbl, work 2, p3tog, work 28 sts—122 sts.

Work 2 rows in pattern as set. Cast off.

Playful, faux-tortoise buttons were chosen for their claw shape, the perfect finishing touch for Kitty!

FINISHING

Turn the hem to the inside and slip stitch in place.

Button Band

Using the smaller needles and yarn (A), with RS facing, pick up and knit 60 (62, 66) sts from the neck to the bottom of the hem at left center front.

Work 8 rows in Moss St., then knit 1 row to form fold line.

Starting on a RS (knit) row, work a further 7 rows in Stockinette St. and cast off.

Buttonhole Band

Work as for Button Band, working 3 buttonholes on rows 4 and 5 of Moss and Stockinette sts. as follows:

Moss St.

Row 4 Work 15 (15, 15), cast off 3 sts, (work 13 [14, 15], cast off 3 sts) twice, work 10 (10, 12).

Row 5 Cast on over these sts as you come to them.

Row 6 Work in pattern as set, working tbl on cast-on sts.

Stockinette St.

Row 4 Work 10 (10, 12), cast off 3 sts, (work 13 [14, 15], cast off 3 sts) twice, work 15 (15, 15).

Row 5 Cast on these sts as you come to them.

Row 6 Work in pattern as set, working tbl on cast-on sts.

Collar

With RS facing and using the smaller needles and yarn (A), pick up and knit 100 (104, 108) sts, starting at the top of the Buttonhole Band.

Work 8 rows in Moss St., working the buttonhole on rows 4 and 5 as follows:

Work 3 sts, cast off 3 sts, work to end.

Cast on these sts on the next row, working tbl on the following row.

Knit 1 row to form fold line. Starting on a knit row, work 7 rows in Stockinette St., working the buttonhole on rows 4 and 5 as follows:

Row 4 Work 3 sts, cast off 3 sts, work to end.

Row 5 Cast on over these sts on the next row, working tbl on the following row.

Cast off.

Turn the bands to the inside and slip stitch in place. Turn the Collar to the inside and slip stitch in place.

Sew the side edges of the Collar together, and sew together the side edges of the bands at the hem.

Neaten buttonholes by stitching around the edges, sewing the 2 thicknesses together. Weave in ends. Attach buttons to the Button Band, opposite the buttonholes on the Buttonhole Band.

Grace Cowl

Grace Kelly is the epitome of 1950s style. The Hermès scarves and Pringle twinsets she wore on her honeymoon with Prince Rainier became instant classics. I hope she would have approved of this delicate cowl, inspired by her cool, fragile elegance. It can be worn two ways—with the ruffled edge over the shoulders or, for a more flamboyant look, framing the face in a Tudor-style ruff. The simple drop-stitch rib pattern is distinctive yet discreet, allowing the glorious cashmere yarn to take center stage.

SKILL LEVEL
Intermediate

FINISHED MEASUREMENTS
7½ in. (19 cm) high, 18½ in. (47 cm) around at flat edge, 27 in. (68.5 cm) around at ruffled edge

YARN
Rowan Pure Cashmere DK
122 yd. (112 m) per 25 g ball:
2 balls Violetta 829

NOTIONS
Size 6 U.S. (4 mm) circular needle
or size to obtain gauge
Stitch marker
Tapestry needle

GAUGE
26 sts and 32 rows = 4 in. (10 cm) in Drop-Stitch Rib pattern

TO MAKE COWL
Cast on 120 sts loosely using the Cable Cast-On (p. 117). Place marker and join in the round, taking care not to twist the sts.
Work the Drop-Stitch Rib pattern, rep the 8 sts of pattern 15 times around, as follows:
Round 1 *P2, k1, yo, k1, p2, k2; rep from * around.
Rounds 2–6 *P2, k3, p2, k2; rep from * around.
Round 7 *P2, k1, drop next st and unravel down to yo of first round, k1, p2, k1, yo, k1; rep from * around.
Rounds 8–12 *P2, k2, p2, k3; rep from * around.
Round 13 *P2, k1, yo, k1, p2, k1, drop next st and unravel down to yo of 7th round, k1; rep from * around.
Rep from round 2.
Cont as set for 49 rounds; on the final round, omit the yarn overs.
Work 2 rounds keeping the 2 by 2 rib pattern correct.
Next round *P1, yo, p1, k1, yo, k1; rep from * around.
Next round *P3, k3; rep from * around.
Rep the last round until the work measures 7½ in. (19 cm).

continued on page 92

Next round *P1, drop next st and unravel down to yo of 52nd round, p1, k1, drop next st and unravel down to yo of 52nd round, yo, k1; rep from * around.

Cast off knitwise using the picot point cast-off: Cast off 2 sts, *slip rem st from RH needle onto the LH needle, cast on 2 sts, cast off 4 sts; rep from * to end and fasten off rem st.

FINISHING

Using the tapestry needle, weave in ends securely on the WS.

Press lightly (p. 116) on the WS.

Grace Schematic

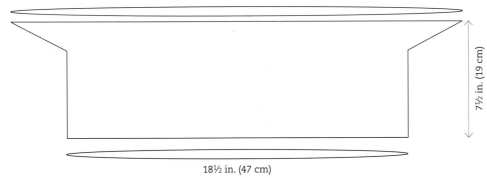

27 in. (68.5 cm)

7½ in. (19 cm)

18½ in. (47 cm)

If your budget doesn't run to cashmere, try a mercerized cotton—soft and silky, with the bonus of cotton's perfect stitch definition.

Brontë Fichu

Wuthering Heights, Emily Brontë's sad tale of tortured and obsessive passion between Heathcliff and Catherine, conjures up potent images of the power of love. The shawl gets several mentions in the novel, so I can well imagine Catherine wearing this fichu. I've combined a delicate fishtail lace with recycled silk and cotton yarn, as the texture and colors remind me of the windswept crags and heather moors of Brontë's Yorkshire. A rewarding lace knit for the incorrigible romantic!

SKILL LEVEL
Experienced

FINISHED MEASUREMENTS
55 in. (139.7 cm) wide, 27½ in. (70 cm) long when blocked

YARN
Rowan Purelife Revive
137 yd. (125 m) per 50 g ball:
2 balls Ironstone 467 (A)
1 ball each Quartz 460 (B), Pink Granite 463 (C), and Marble 466 (D)

NOTIONS
1 pair size 6 U.S. (4 mm) needles
or size to obtain gauge
Size G-6 U.S. (4 mm) crochet hook
Stitch markers
Tapestry needle

GAUGE
20 sts and 24 rows = 4 in. (10 cm) in Fishtail Lace pattern

TO MAKE SHAWL
Using size 6 U.S. (4 mm) needles and yarn (A), cast on 7 sts.
Work the neck edge as follows:
Row 1 (WS) Purl.
Row 2 Knit.
Row 3 P1, yo, p2, yo, pm, p1, yo, p2, yo, p1—11 sts.
Row 4 Knit.
Row 5 P1, yo, p4, yo, pm, p1, yo, p4, yo, p1—15 sts.
Row 6 Knit.
Row 7 P1, yo, p6, yo, pm, p1, yo, p6, yo, p1—19 sts.
Row 8 Knit.
Row 9 P1, yo, p8, yo, pm, p1, yo, p8, yo, p1—23 sts.
Row 10 Knit.
Row 11 P1, yo, p10, yo, pm, p1, yo, p10, yo, p1—27 sts.
Row 12 Knit.
Change to yarn (D) and cont to work the Fishtail Lace pattern as follows, changing colors every 16 rows to end—(C), (B), (A), (D), (C), (B), (A)—and keeping the lace pattern correct as you inc, introducing another whole pattern as soon as you have the sts—140 rows.
Row 13 and all WS rows Inc 4 sts as set.
Row 14 K3, ssk, k3tbl, yo, k1, yo, k3tbl, k2tog, k3, ssk, k3tbl, yo, k1, yo, k3tbl, k2tog, k3.
Row 16 K4, ssk, k2tbl, yo, k1, yo, ssk, yo, k2tbl, k2tog, k5, ssk, k2tbl, yo, k1, yo, ssk, yo, k2tbl, k2tog, k4.
Row 18 K5, ssk, k1tbl, yo, k1, (yo, ssk) twice, yo, k1tbl, k2tog, k7, ssk, k1tbl, yo, k1, (yo, ssk) twice, yo, k1tbl, k2tog, k5.

continued on page 97

Row 20 K6, ssk, yo, k1, (yo, ssk) 3 times, yo, k2tog, k9, ssk, yo, k1, (yo, ssk) 3 times, yo, k2tog, k6.

Row 22 K7, ssk, k3tbl, yo, k1, yo, k3tbl, k2tog, k11, ssk, k3tbl, yo, k1, yo, k3tbl, k2tog, k7.

Row 24 K8, ssk, k2tbl, yo, k1, yo, ssk, yo, k2tbl, k2tog, k13, ssk, k2tbl, yo, k1, yo, ssk, yo, k2tbl, k2tog, k8.

Row 26 K9, ssk, k1tbl, yo, k1, (yo, ssk) twice, yo, k1tbl, k2tog, k15, ssk, k1tbl, yo, k1, (yo, ssk) twice, yo, k1tbl, k2tog, k9.

Row 28 K10, ssk, yo, k1, (yo, ssk) 3 times, yo, k2tog, k17, ssk, yo, k1, (yo, ssk) 3 times, yo, k2tog, k10.

Row 30 K11, ssk, k3tbl, yo, k1, yo, k3tbl, k2tog, k19, ssk, k3tbl, yo, k1, yo, k3tbl, k2tog, k11.

Row 32 K12, ssk, k2tbl, yo, k1, yo, ssk, yo, k2tbl, k2tog, k21, ssk, k2tbl, yo, k1, yo, ssk, yo, k2tbl, k2tog, k12.

Row 34 K2, (ssk, k1tbl, yo, k1, [yo, ssk] twice, yo, k1tbl, k2tog) 3 times, k1, (ssk, k1tbl, yo, k1, [yo, ssk] twice, yo, k1tbl, k2tog) 3 times, k2.

For rows 36–140, keep stripes correct as set and keep Fishtail patt. correct as set, using basic 8-row repeat as guide:

Fishtail Lace

Multiple of 11 sts.

Note: Pattern is written out below so that you can keep pattern correct after row 34.

Rows 1, 3, 5, 7 purl

Row 2 *ssk, k3tbl, yo, k1, yo, k3tbl, k2tog; rep from *

Row 4 *ssk, k2tbl, yo, k1, yo, ssk, yo, k2tbl, k2tog; rep from *

Row 6 *ssk, k1tbl, yo, k1, (yo, ssk) twice, yo, k1tbl, k2tog; rep from *

Row 8 *ssk, yo, k1, (yo, ssk) three times, yo, k2tog; rep from *

Note: Row 36 use Row 8 as its template

When all reps have been worked and the 9th stripe in yarn (A) is complete, work a further purl inc row—141 rows.

Cast off all 283 sts.

FINISHING

Securely weave ends into like colors.

Using the crochet hook and yarn (A), work a Shell St. edging around the Shawl as follows: Sl 1, *skip 2 sts, 5 dc in next st, skip 2 sts, sl 1; rep from * to end.

Brontë Schematic

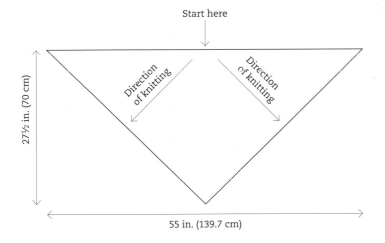

Sweater clips, particularly vintage-style ones, are great retro accessories that keep shawlettes prettily in place.

Mantilla Shawlette

Inspired by the exquisite mantillas in the paintings of Goya and Velazquez, this piece is a wonderful way to wrap up and look glamorous at the same time. Fashionable way back in the 17th and 18th centuries, they're on track for a revival since the royal wedding of Prince William and Kate, when the now Duchess of Cambridge wore a beautiful lace mantilla as her bridal veil. Worked in the round for easier knitting and extra coziness, the unusual circular lace pattern is beautiful on both sides, creating a true heirloom piece.

SKILL LEVEL
Experienced

FINISHED MEASUREMENTS
22 in. (56 cm) high, 44 in. (112 cm) around

YARN
Rowan Kidsilk Haze
229 yd. (210 m) per 25 g ball:
3 balls Marmalade 596

NOTIONS
Size 7 U.S. (4.5 mm) extra-long circular needle *or size to obtain gauge*
Stitch marker
Tapestry needle

GAUGE
20 sts and 26 rows = 4 in. (10 cm) in Circle Lace Chart pattern

TO MAKE SHAWLETTE
Cast on 216 sts loosely using the Cable Cast-On (p. 117). Place marker and join in the round, taking care not to twist the sts.
Work the Circle Lace Chart pattern, repeating the 12 sts 18 times around.
Cont for 120 rows or until work measures approx 18 in. (45.7 cm), ending on row 12 or 24.
Cast off as follows: K1, *pass this st back to LH needle and k2tog; rep from * across row.

FINISHING
Cast on 8 sts and work the Lace Edging to fit around the top of the Shawlette as follows:
Row 1 (WS) Sl 1, k1, *yo, p2tog, (k1, p1, k1) into next st; rep from *—12 sts.
Row 2 (K3, yo, p2tog) twice, k2.
Row 3 Sl 1, k1, (yo, p2tog, k3) twice.
Row 4 Cast off first 2 sts knitwise (1 st on RH needle), yo, p2tog, cast off next 2 sts knitwise (4 sts on RH needle), yo, p2tog, k2—8 sts.

continued on page 100

Rep these 4 rows to the required length, ending on row 4.

Oversew the edging in place on the inside of the Shawlette, then sew together the cast-on and cast-off edges.

Work and attach a similar edging around the base of the Shawlette. Securely weave in ends.

Mantilla Schematic

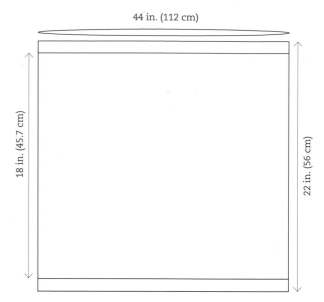

Circle Lace Chart

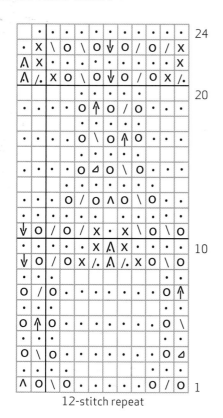

12-stitch repeat

☐	K
·	P
O	Yo
/	K2tog
\	Ssk
/.	P2tog
X	No stitch
↑	S2kpo
↓	(K1b, k1) in 1 st, then insert LH needle behind vertical strand running downward from between 2 sts just made, k1b into this strand to make third st
Λ	Sk2po
◿	K3tog
Λ	P3tog

Note: As you are knitting in the round, all chart rows are read from right to left.

Whether worn as a shawl or head scarf, Mantilla's pattern creates a shawlette that is as lightweight as actual lace.

Vamp Boa

Evoking the glamour of Hollywood film stars like Marilyn Monroe, Mae West, and Jean Harlow, this frothy concoction is guaranteed to lift your spirits as soon as you put it on. An easy stockinette knit in a kid mohair and silk blend, the layered pieces are ruched together down the center, then the seam is adorned with silk ribbon. A very wearable piece, this boa is sure to turn heads at any party.

SKILL LEVEL
Easy

FINISHED MEASUREMENTS
6 in. (15.2 cm) wide, 80 in. (203 cm) long when flat
6 in. (15.2 cm) wide, 48 in. (122 cm) long when ruched

YARN
Rowan Kidsilk Night
227 yd. (208 m) per 25 g ball:
2 balls Moonlight 608 (A)
Rowan Kidsilk Aura
82 yd. (75 m) per 25 g ball:
3 balls Vintage 757 (B)

NOTIONS
1 pair size 8 U.S. (5 mm) needles *or size to obtain gauge*
Stitch markers
Tapestry needle
4 yd. (4 m) silver shirring elastic
3 yd. (4 m) silk ribbon, 5 mm wide

GAUGE
16 sts and 24 rows = 4 in. (10 cm) in Stockinette Stitch (p. 121)

Note
Slip the first stitch purlwise and knit into the back of the last stitch on every row.

TO MAKE BOA
Using yarn (A), cast on 24 sts and work in Stockinette St. until the piece measures 80 in. (203 cm), ending on a WS row. Cast off loosely.
Make a second piece in the same way using yarn (B).

FINISHING
Press lightly (p. 116) under a damp cloth on the WS.

Stitch Pieces Together
Place markers after sts 11 and 13 at the beg and end of each piece.
Place the 2 pieces, WS together, and work 2 lines of shirring elastic in a running st through the Boa pieces between markers. Work the first elastic lengthwise along st 11, and the second elastic lengthwise along st 13.

continued on page 104

Ruche evenly until Boa measures 48 in. (122 cm) long and then fasten off.

Thread the ribbon alternately through the sts down the center, between the 2 lines of elastic. Secure ends with a knot and leave the spare 7 in. (18 cm) of ribbon to finish.

Vamp Schematic

6 in.
(15.2 cm)

80 in. (203 cm) flat
48 in. (122 cm) ruched

Thoughts on Color

Color has a powerful effect on our everyday lives. Here are some fun tips for choosing just the right color for your Vamp Boa.

Red is a symbol of protection and caution in many cultures. It is powerful and passionate.

Blue is at once uplifting, relaxing, serene, and inspiring.

Yellow is the brightest color in the spectrum. It lifts the spirits and brings a sense of joy.

Green is nature's hallmark, said to encourage good fortune and healing.

Purple is a symbol of royalty, wealth, ritual, creativity, and eccentricity.

Neutrals such as ivory, taupe, and buff, borrow their hue from the natural world and are symbolic of wholeness and unity.

Metallics such as silver, gold, bronze, and copper bring life and oomph to the world around us, and in many cultures are thought to deflect the "evil eye" and inspire creativity.

Boas are versatile and can be worn as a collar, scarf, or lariat. Indulge in silk ribbon to lace your boa: The shine and texture of real silk is perfectly lovely against the yarn.

Treasure Jabot

Bowl your friends over in this stunning pure silk jabot. Originally made of cambric or lace, the jabot has had many incarnations over hundreds of years, from military and traditional Scottish dress to neckwear for judges—and also pirates. I love pattern-on-pattern, and entrelac works well with frills to emphasize texture. However, despite looking intricate, this pattern is a straightforward knit once you get the hang of entrelac. The frills are a movable feast; I've got three, but you can knit more or less, depending on how frivolous you're feeling.

SKILL LEVEL
Intermediate

FINISHED MEASUREMENTS
3 in. (7.5 cm) high, 39 in. (100 cm) wide without frills, 46 in. (117 cm) with frills

YARN
Rowan Pure Silk DK
137 yd. (125 m) per 50 g ball:
2 balls Firefly 162

NOTIONS
1 pair size 5 U.S. (3.75 mm) needles, *or size to obtain gauge,* plus 1 extra needle
Size F-5 U.S. (3.25 mm) crochet hook
2 stitch holders

GAUGE
24 sts and 28 rows = 4 in. (10 cm) in Stockinette Stitch (p. 121)

TO MAKE JABOT
Loosely cast on 132 sts and work in entrelac as follows:

Base triangles
First base triangle *P2, turn, k2, turn, p3, turn.
Cont in this way, purling 1 st more from the LH needle each time, until there are 6 sts on the RH needle. Do not turn. Rep from * 21 times—22 base triangles.

First row of blocks
First edging triangle K2, turn, p2 turn, kfb, then skpo, turn, p3, turn, kfb, k1, then skpo, turn, p4, turn. Cont in this way, dec 1 st from the base triangles on knit rows each time until *kfb, k3, skpo* has been worked. Do not turn; leave these 6 sts.
Blocks *Pick up and knit 6 sts from the row ends of the 1st base triangle, turn, p6, turn, k5, skpo, turn, p6. Cont in this way until all sts of the 1st base triangle have been decreased. Do not turn. Rep from * for 20 more blocks across the row, picking up sts between the base triangles.

continued on page 109

For a touch of classic style, consider adding a vintage gold tiepin horizontally across the top of the frills.

Second edging triangle Pick up and k6 sts from the row ends of the last base triangle, turn, p2tog, p4, turn, k5, turn. P2tog, p3, turn, k4.
Cont in this way, dec at the beg of every purl row until 1 st rem, turn, slip st onto the RH needle.

Second Row of Blocks (No Side Triangles)

Blocks *P1, pick up and purl 5 sts, turn, k6, turn. P5, p2tog, turn, k6.
Cont in this way until all sts of the 1st row of blocks have been decreased. Do not turn. Work 21 more blocks in this way, picking up 6 sts.

Third Row of Blocks

Work as for 1st row (including edging triangles), working into the 2nd row of blocks instead of into the base triangles.

Closing Triangles

P1, *pick up and purl 5 sts from row-ends of the 1st side triangle, turn, k6, turn. P2tog, p3, p2tog, turn, k5, turn. P2tog, p2, p2tog, turn, k4, turn.
Cont in this way until *turn, k2* has been worked, turn, p1, p2tog, turn, k2, turn, p3tog—1 st rem.
Rep from * to complete the other 21 closing triangles.
Fasten off rem st.

Frills (Make 2)

**Cast on 50 sts and knit 2 rows. Then work 8 rows in Stockinette St.
Next row K1, *k3tog; rep from * to last st, k1—18 sts. **
Cont working these sts for a further 8 rows in Stockinette St., then leave on holder.
Rep from ** to **, then place the 2nd frill on top of the 1st frill and, using the 3rd needle, purl the front and back needles together on the next row—18 sts.
Cont working these sts for a further 8 rows in Stockinette St., then leave on holder.
Rep from ** to ** once more, then place the new frill on top of first 2 frills and join together as before, using 3 needles—18 sts.
With RS facing, pick up and knit 18 sts along the side edge of Jabot. Then place together the right sides of a joined frill and jabot and work a Three-Needle Bind-Off (p. 121). Attach the other frill to other end in the same way.

FINISHING

Securely weave in ends. Press lightly (p. 116) on the WS.
With RS facing, work 1 row of single crochet (p. 120) along the cast-on and cast-off edges.

Treasure Schematic

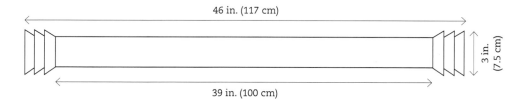

46 in. (117 cm)

39 in. (100 cm)

3 in. (7.5 cm)

Fizz Capelet

Knit some sparkle into your life with this glam capelet. Practice your short rows with each flare on this edge-to-edge piece, adding the beads as you knit. It sounds like a lot to do, but the pattern is all stockinette, and once you've threaded the beads, they're easy to add to the work. You'll be cracking the bubbly before you know it!

SKILL LEVEL
Intermediate

FINISHED MEASUREMENTS
Small: 18¼ in. (46.5 cm) wide at neck edge, 12 in. (30.5 cm) long; to fit bust 32-34 in. (81-86 cm)
Medium: 19½ in. (49.5 cm) wide at neck edge, 12½ in. (31.7 cm) long; to fit bust 36-38 in. (91.5-96.5 cm)
Large: 20 in. (51 cm) wide at neck edge, 13 in. (33 cm) long; to fit bust 40-42 in. (101-106.5 cm)
Pattern is written for size Small, with Medium and Large instructions in parentheses where necessary.

YARN
Rowan Siena 4 Ply
153 yd. (140 m) per 50 g ball:
4 (5, 5) balls Celadan 669

NOTIONS
1 pair size 2 U.S. (3 mm) needles *or size to obtain gauge*
Stitch markers
Approx 1,000 size 8 clear beads (I used Debbie Abrahams #34.)
Beading needle
Tapestry needle

GAUGE
28 sts and 38 rows = 4 in. (10 cm) in Stockinette Stitch (p. 121)

SPECIAL ABBREVIATION
Bead 1
Bring yarn to RS of work, slide bead up to the stitch just worked, slip next stitch purlwise, and take yarn to WS of work, leaving the bead on the RS in front of the slipped stitch.

Notes
Thread beads onto each ball before starting to knit.
For size Small, thread 171 beads on the first ball, 117 beads on the second ball, 122 beads on the third ball, and 87 beads on the fourth ball to finish the body of Capelet; thread an extra 150 beads on fourth ball to make the collar. To allow for variation in yardage, add a few more beads to each ball.
For sizes Medium and Large, the number of beads needed should be similar, as fewer rows will be knit from each ball. However, to be on the safe side, thread an extra 20 beads on each ball.
Capelet is worked in one piece sideways from front edge to front edge.

continued on page 112

TO MAKE CAPELET
Cast on 83 (87, 91) sts with the first ball
of prepared yarn.

Band
Work the band as follows:

Row 1 *K1, bead 1, k1, p1; rep from *
to last 3 sts, k1, bead 1, k1.

Row 2 *K1, p1; rep from * to last st, k1.

Row 3 *K1, p1, k1, bead 1; rep from *
to last 3 sts, k1, p1, k1.

Row 4 Work as for row 2.

Row 5 Work as for row 1.

Row 6 K1, p1, k1, p1, k1, p1, k1, purl to end.

Capelet
Work 12 (12, 14) rows in Stockinette St. as follows:

Row 1 K1, p1, k1, bead 1, k1, p1, k1, knit to end.

Row 2 Purl to last 7 sts, k1, p1, k1, p1, k1, p1, k1.

Row 3 K1, bead 1, k1, p1, k1, bead 1, k1, knit to end.

Row 4 Purl to last 7 sts, k1, p1, k1, p1, k1, p1, k1.

For Small and Medium sizes
Rep these 4 rows twice—12 rows.

For Large size
Rep these 4 rows twice, then work rows 1 and
2—14 rows.

Place markers after first 7 sts, then every
5 sts 14 times.

Shape Capelet
Note: Each set of 2 rows consists of the sts up to
the wrap (first row), and the sts purled back
(second row). For complete instructions on
wrapping a stitch, see p. 121.

For Large size
Keep the Moss St. pattern (p. 119) correct by
starting as for Row 3.

Work the short row shaping as follows**:

Rows 1 & 2 K1, p1, k1, bead 1, k1, p1, k1, k5,
w & t, p5, work 7 sts in Moss St.

Rows 3 & 4 K1, bead 1, k1, p1, k1, bead 1, k1, k10
(picking up wrap on 6th st, and knitting it together
with the st it wraps), w & t, p10, work 7 sts
in Moss St.

Note: On subsequent RS rows, wrap next st before
turning, picking up wrap on foll RS row.

Rows 5 & 6 K1, p1, k1, bead 1, k1, p1, k1, k15,
w & t, p15, work 7 sts in Moss St.

Rows 7 & 8 K1, bead 1, k1, p1, k1, bead 1, k1, k20,
w & t, p20, work 7 sts in Moss St.

Rows 9 & 10 K1, p1, k1, bead 1, k1, p1, k1, k25,
w & t, p25, work 7 sts in Moss St.

Rows 11 & 12 K1, bead 1, k1, p1, k1, bead 1, k1,
k30, w & t, p30, work 7 sts in Moss St.

Rows 13 & 14 K1, p1, k1, bead 1, k1, p1, k1, k35,
w & t, p35, work 7 sts in Moss St.

continued on page 115

Fizz Schematic

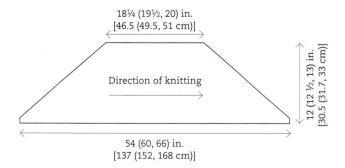

18¼ (19½, 20) in.
[46.5 (49.5, 51 cm)]

Direction of knitting

12 (12 ½, 13) in.
[30.5 (31.7, 33 cm)]

54 (60, 66) in.
[137 (152, 168 cm)]

*Add more glitz by emphasizing
the godets. Outline each one with
an embroidered chain stitch,
adding extra beads evenly every
few stitches as you go.*

Rows 15 & 16 K1, bead 1, k1, p1, k1, bead 1, k1, k40, w & t, p40, work 7 sts in Moss St.

Rows 17 & 18 K1, p1, k1, bead 1, k1, p1, k1, k45, w & t, p45, work 7 sts in Moss St.

Rows 19 & 20 K1, bead 1, k1, p1, k1, bead 1, k1, k50, w & t, p50, work 7 sts in Moss St.

Rows 21 & 22 K1, p1, k1, bead 1, k1, p1, k1, k55, w & t, p55, work 7 sts in Moss St.

Rows 23 & 24 K1, bead 1, k1, p1, k1, bead 1, k1, k60, w & t, p60, work 7 sts in Moss St.

Rows 25 & 26 K1, p1, k1, bead 1, k1, p1, k1, k65, w & t, p65, work 7 sts in Moss St.

Rows 27 & 28 K1, bead 1, k1, p1, k1, bead 1, k1, k70, w & t, p70, work 7 sts in Moss St.

Note: On subsequent rows the wraps will be picked up on final row.

Rows 29 & 30 K1, p1, k1, bead 1, k1, p1, k1, k65, w & t, p65, work 7 sts in Moss St.

Rows 31 & 32 K1, bead 1, k1, p1, k1, bead 1, k1, k60, w & t, p60, work 7 sts in Moss St.

Rows 33 & 34 K1, p1, k1, bead 1, k1, p1, k1, k55, w & t, p55, work 7 sts in Moss St.

Rows 35 & 36 K1, bead 1, k1, p1, k1, bead 1, k1, k50, w & t, p50, work 7 sts in Moss St.

Rows 37 & 38 K1, p1, k1, bead 1, k1, p1, k1, k45, w & t, p45, work 7 sts in Moss St.

Rows 39 & 40 K1, bead 1, k1, p1, k1, bead 1, k1, k40, w & t, p40, work 7 sts in Moss St.

Rows 41 & 42 K1, p1, k1, bead 1, k1, p1, k1, k35, w & t, p35, work 7 sts in Moss St.

Rows 43 & 44 K1, bead 1, k1, p1, k1, bead 1, k1, w & t, p30, work 7 sts in Moss St.

Rows 45 & 46 K1, p1, k1, bead 1, k1, p1, k1, k25, w & t, p25, work 7 sts in Moss St.

Rows 47 & 48 K1, bead 1, k1, p1, k1, bead 1, k1, k20, w & t, p20, work 7 sts in Moss St.

Rows 49 & 50 K1, p1, k1, bead 1, k1, p1, k1, k15, w & t, p15, work 7 sts in Moss St.

Rows 51 & 52 K1, bead 1, k1, p1, k1, bead 1, k1, k10, w & t, p10, work 7 sts in Moss St.

Rows 53 & 54 K1, p1, k1, bead 1, k1, p1, k1, k5, w & t, p5, work 7 sts in Moss St.

Row 55 K1, bead 1, k1, p1, k1, bead 1, k1, k76 (80, 84), picking up all the wraps.

Row 56 P76 (80, 84), work 7 sts in Moss St. Work 28 (24, 20) rows in Stockinette St., keeping the beaded Moss St. border correct ****. Rep from ** to **** 5 (6, 7) more times, keeping the beaded Moss St. border correct, and finishing the last rep by working 12 (12, 14) rows in Stockinette St.

Second Band

Work the Second Band as for rows 1–5 of the first—511 (571, 627) total project rows. Cast off.

FINISHING (COLLAR)

With RS facing, pick up and knit 119 (127, 131) sts around the neck edge. Work in Moss St. for 10 rows as follows:

Row 1 (WS) *K1, p1; rep from * to last st, k1.

Row 2 *K1, bead 1, k1, p1; rep from * to last 3 sts, k1, bead 1, k1.

Row 3 *K1, p1; rep from * to last st, k1.

Row 4 *K1, p1, k1, bead 1; rep from * to last 3 sts, k1, p1, k1.

Rep these 4 rows, then work the first 2 rows. Knit 1 row to form a fold line, then work in Stockinette St. for 1¼ in. (3 cm), then cast off kwise. Turn down the collar and slip stitch it in place on inside. Sew the side edges of the collar together. Work 48 (50, 52) in. (122, 127, 132 cm) of I-cord (p. 119), leaving a long tail at both ends. Mark the center and place it at the center back of the cape, at the point where the collar starts. Slip stitch the I-cord in place around the neckline, allowing the I-cord to hang at each end for tying. Weave ends into the side edges. Attach a loop of 9 beads to each end of the I-cord.

APPENDIX I

Techniques and Stitches

HERE YOU'LL FIND TECHNIQUES AND STITCH PATTERNS you need to create your very own sweet shawlettes.

Attaching Beads

For attaching beads, I prefer the slip stitch method, as it ensures that the bead stays on the right side of the work.

On a RS row, work to the position of the beaded stitch. Bring the yarn forward to the front of the work and push a bead down the yarn so that it lies against the needle at the front of the work. Slip the next stitch purlwise, leaving the bead in front of the slipped stitch. Take the yarn to the back and continue to work as normal.

On a WS row, work to the position of the bead, take the yarn to the back of the work and place the bead so that it lies on RS of work against the needle. Slip the next stitch purlwise, leaving the bead behind the slipped stitch. Take the yarn to the front and continue to purl as set.

NOTE: The Big Eye needle is wonderful for threading the beads. As its name suggests, it's one gigantic flexible eye. If you can't find one, then thread a fine needle with about 8 in. (20 cm) of cotton thread and knot the two ends together. Thread the yarn through the loop of cotton thread and off you go.

Backward Loop Cast-On

This simple cast-on is useful for casting on stitches in the middle of a row. It's sometimes used for making a stitch between stitches.

Make a backward loop and place it on the needle. Repeat as many times as required.

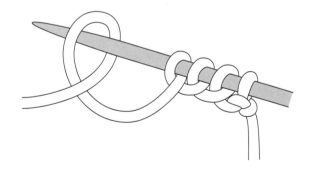

Blocking and Pressing

Never underestimate the power of blocking and pressing! Small mistakes often become invisible when a piece is well presented. Some projects need pressing more than others, so I've included specific instructions to press in some projects.

Before blocking, neaten the selvages by sewing or weaving in all the ends along the sides or along color joins where appropriate. Then, using pins, block each piece of knitting to shape— this also gives you an opportunity to check the measurements. Gently press each piece on the WS, omitting ribbing, using a warm iron and a damp pressing cloth. Take special care with the edges.

Cable Cast-On

This is a useful cast-on when stitches need to be added within your work.

Make a slip knot on the LH needle. Working into this knot's loop, k1 st and place it on the LH needle.

Insert the RH needle between the last 2 sts. From this position, k1 st and place it on the LH needle. Rep this step to cast on each additional st.

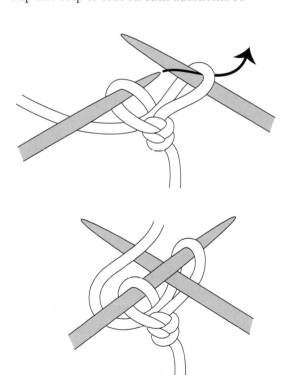

Cables

Cabling is a simply a way of crossing one set of stitches over another set and looks best when worked against a contrasting background stitch, like working a Stockinette Stitch cable on a reverse Stockinette Stitch background. Basic cables are worked by placing the first set of stitches on a cable needle and holding them at the back or front of your knitting, depending on whether you want the crossing to slope toward the right or left. Holding the stitches at the front will result in a left-sloping cable, and holding them at the back will yield a right-sloping cable. For example, here's a 4-stitch cable that slopes to the left:

On a RS row, work to the position of the cable and sl the next 2 sts onto the cable needle, holding it at the *front* of the work.

Working behind the cable needle, knit the next 2 sts from the LH needle.

Now knit the 2 sts from the cable needle to create a crossover to the left.

Chart Reading

When knitting back and forth, charts are read from right to left on RS rows and from left to right on WS rows. Charts can begin with a RS or WS row; this will be indicated by where Row 1 is situated on the chart. For instance, if Row 1 is on the left, then the chart starts with a WS row, if it is on the right, it starts with a RS row. In circular knitting, all rows are RS rows and every row is read from right to left.

Every square (or rectangle) in a chart represents 1 stitch horizontally and 1 row vertically. The symbols inside each square represent either stitches (knit, purl, cable, and so on) or colors (in intarsia or two-color stranded knitting). When working with several colors, it's good to tape a small piece of each color alongside its symbol so you have a constant reminder of which yarn to use.

To keep track of your place in the chart, use a premade line finder or make one yourself by taking a strip of card or plastic the width of the chart and cut a long slit into it, approximately the size of a row. This window can then be moved up the chart as you knit, masking the rows you've knitted and highlighting the one you're working on. If the size of a chart is too small for comfortable reading as printed in the book, enlarge it using a photocopier before you start the project.

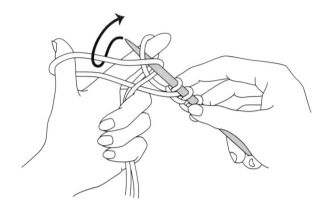

Continental Cast-On

Make a slip knot for the initial st, at a distance from the end of the yarn about 1 in. (2.5 cm) for each st to be cast on. Arrange both ends of the yarn in the left hand as shown. Bring the needle under the front strand of the thumb loop, up over the front strand of the index finger loop, catching the yarn on the needle.

Bring the same needle under the front of the thumb loop. Slip the thumb out of the loop, and use it to adjust the tension on the new st—1 st cast on.

Rep this process until all the sts are cast on.

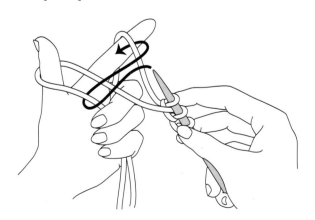

Entrelac

Entrelac is a fabulous technique for adding both color and texture to your knitting. Take a look at Harlequin Cape (p. 46) or Treasure Jabot (p. 106) for full instructions on how to get up to speed with this highly effective yet simple skill, which belongs in every knitter's portfolio.

Fair Isle (Two-Color Stranded Knitting)

Many knitters remain in awe of this technique, but once you have mastered Stockinette Stitch, you are ready for Fair Isle. It's just a matter of organizing your yarn and making sure you don't pull the yarn too tightly to maintain elasticity in the knitted fabric. The nonworking yarn is carried loosely on the wrong side, either woven in or stranded.

In my workshops, I usually teach the two-handed method, but this involves working simultaneously with the British method (throwing the yarn), in which the working yarn is held in the right hand, and the Continental method (picking the yarn), in which it is held in the left hand. This produces an even, pleasing effect and is wonderfully rhythmic when working in the round, where all rows are knit rows.

However, when knitting back and forth, I've found that a lot of knitters have a problem with the tension on the purl side. A speedy and even alternative is to use either circular or double-pointed needles and work across the row, *knitting* every Color A stitch and *slipping* (purlwise) every Color B stitch. Do not turn the work at the end of the row, but instead slide the stitches back to the right hand point of the needle, drop Color A, pick up Color B and work every stitch that should be Color B, *slipping* every stitch that was previously worked in Color A. Then turn the work and proceed in the same way on the purl side. When working in the round, work one round with Color A and then one round with Color B to complete each single row. If you always smoothly stretch out the slipped stitches on the right-hand needle before stranding the yarn, this method makes it easy to control the tension of the strands and avoids any puckering of the fabric. Do not strand the yarn over more than 3 stitches.

Garter Stitch
Knit all rows or purl all rows.

Garter Stitch in the Round
Round 1 Knit.
Round 2 Purl.
Rep these 2 rounds.

I-Cord
Cast on 3 sts using a double-pointed needle, *slide these sts to the other end of the needle, then knit them using the yarn brought around from the other end. Rep from * to end.

Intarsia
A way of getting as many colors as you're able to handle into one row, this technique was once called picture knitting. It can create wonderful designs and it's not difficult, per se, but it can be fiddly and therefore off-putting to new knitters. Try it out on the border of the Madame Alfred Shawlette (p. 10) or take the plunge with the Kitty Capelet (p. 84)—if you find you enjoy the process, there's a huge pot of gold at the end of this knitting rainbow!

If the design has a background color, use separate balls of yarn for each of the contrast colors, stranding or weaving the main color behind. This cuts down on the number of ends to weave in later and gives the contrast colors a slightly raised effect, which helps define the pattern.

For intarsia with random shapes, use a separate length of yarn for each color every time it occurs, twisting the two colors around each other at the start and finish to avoid creating holes in the knitting. To eliminate tangles, wrap each length around a bobbin and let it dangle on the back of the work or use short lengths of yarn (no longer than 24 in. (61 cm) and straighten at the end of each row.

Moss Stitch
Row 1 *K1, p1; rep from * to end.
On all subsequent rows, purl the knit sts and knit the purl sts.

Picking Up Stitches Around a Neckline
To get a professional finish on a neckline, it's important to pick up and knit evenly, with no bunching or stretching of stitches. Sometimes, due to the design of a pattern, stitches are left live at the center back and/or center front, but unless

the pattern calls for this, it's generally best to cast off. The reason for this is that all the stress of the garment when worn will be falling away from the center back neck; therefore, necklines tend to stretch and become bigger than intended. One way of countering this is to do a firm cast-off at the center back and front neck edges.

To pick up a stitch from a cast-off edge, hold the knitting with the right side toward you, insert the needle under an edge stitch, wrap the yarn around, and pull a loop through to make a stitch.

Pick up the number of stitches indicated in the pattern, and remember that the next row will be a WS row.

Selvage Edges

Always work a selvage on every row when possible. This helps prevent curl and makes finishing easier (especially when sewing pieces together using a mattress stitch), as the resulting notches can be matched. There are many different selvage stitches, but old habits die hard, and I usually use the beaded selvage my grandmother taught me:

Sl the first st knitwise and knit into the back of the last st on every row.

Another good stitch to use is the chain selvage, which is great for backstitch seams and also helps when picking up stitches or working crochet edges:

RS rows Sl the first st knitwise and knit the last st.
WS rows Sl the first stitch purlwise and purl the last st.

Take time to experiment and find the selvage stitch that works for you.

Single Crochet (U.K. Double Crochet)

I often use crochet to finish off a shawlette. In this book I use the U.S. term *single crochet*; U.K. knitters should remember that terminology for basic crochet stitches like single crochet and double crochet in the U.S. translates into double crochet and treble crochet, respectively, in the U.K.

Make a slip knot to begin.

Insert the hook into the next st.

Yo and pull a loop through the next st indicated in the pattern—2 loops are on the hook.

Yo and pull a loop through both loops on the hook, 1 single crochet completed.

Rep steps 1–3 as instructed in the pattern.

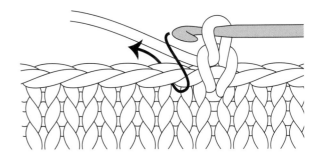

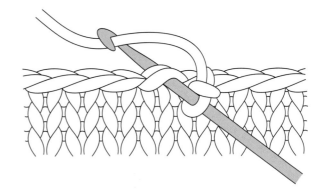

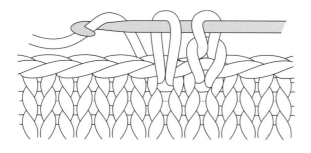

Stockinette Stitch

Knit on RS rows and purl on WS rows.

Stockinette Stitch in the Round

Knit every round.

Three-Needle Bind-Off

This is a neat way of joining seams on the inside or decoratively on the outside, especially if the shoulder shaping uses short rows.

Place the work RS together, with the back sts on 1 needle and front sts on another. *Work 2 tog (1 from front needle and 1 from back needle). Rep from * once.

Cast off the first st over the second st. Continue to work 2 sts tog (1 front st and 1 back st) and cast off across.

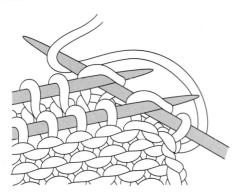

Wrapping a Stitch

On a knit row:

With yarn in back, sl the next st as if to purl. Bring the yarn to the front of the work and sl the st back to the LH needle. Turn the work.

Work the row as instructed in the pattern, and when you come to the wrap on the following knit row, make it less visible by knitting it together with the stitch it wraps.

Yarn Information

Numbers in brackets correspond with yarn weight symbols in the Standard Yarn Weight System chart, p. 124.

Rowan Big Wool
87 yd. (80 m) per 100 g ball:
100% merino wool
[CYCA 6]

Rowan Cashsoft 4 Ply
175 yd. (160 m) per 50 g ball:
57% extra-fine merino, 33% acrylic microfiber,
10% cashmere, [CYCA 1]

Rowan Cashsoft DK
126 yd. (115 m) per 50 g ball:
57% extra-fine merino, 33% acrylic microfiber,
10% cashmere, [CYCA 3]

Rowan Chunky Chenille
151 yd. (140 m) per 100 g ball:
100% cotton, [CYCA 4]

Rowan Cocoon
126 yd. (115 m) per 100 g ball:
80% merino wool, 20% kid mohair
[CYCA 5]

Rowan Colourscape Chunky
175 yd. (160 m) per 100 g skein:
100% lambswool, [CYCA 5]

Rowan Denim
109 yd. (100 m) per 50 g ball:
100% cotton, [CYCA 4]

Rowan Drift
87 yd. (80 m) per 100 g ball:
100% merino wool, [CYCA 6]

Rowan Felted Tweed DK
191 yd. (175 m) per 50 g ball:
50% merino, 25% alpaca, 25% viscose
[CYCA 3]

Rowan Kidsilk Aura
82 yd. (75 m) per 25 g ball:
75% kid mohair, 25% silk, [CYCA 4]

Rowan Kidsilk Haze
229 yd. (210 m) per 25 g ball:
70% super kid mohair, 30% silk, [CYCA 4]

Rowan Kidsilk Night
227 yd. (208 m) per 25 g ball:
67% super kid mohair, 18% silk,
10% polyester, 5% nylon, [CYCA 3]

Rowan Lenpur Linen
126 yd. (115 m) per 50 g ball:
75% VI Lenpur (viscose), 25% linen, [CYCA 3]

Rowan Lima
109 yd. (100 m) per 50 g ball:
84% baby alpaca, 8% merino wool, 8% nylon
[CYCA 4]

Rowan Milk Cotton Fine
164 yd. (150 m) per 50 g ball:
70% cotton, 30% milk protein, [CYCA 1]

Rowan Mulberry Silk
164 yd. (150 m) per 50 g hank:
100% mulberry silk, [CYCA 1]

Rowan Pure Cashmere DK
122 yd. (112 m) per 25 g ball:
100% cashmere, [CYCA 3]

Rowan Purelife Renew
82 yd. (75 m) per 50 g ball:
93% recycled wool, 7% polyamide, [CYCA 5]

Rowan Purelife Revive
137 yd. (125 m) per 50 g ball:
36% recycled silk, 36% recycled cotton,
28% recycled viscose, [CYCA 3]

Rowan Pure Silk DK
137 yd. (125 m) per 50 g ball:
100% silk, [CYCA 3]

Rowan Shimmer
191 yd. (175 m) per 25 g ball:
60% cupro, 40% polyester, [CYCA 1]

Rowan Siena 4 Ply
153 yd. (140 m) per 50 g ball:
100% mercerized cotton, [CYCA 1]

Rowan Silk Twist
93 yd. (85 m) per 50 g ball:
53% silk, 30% wool, 12% superkid mohair,
5% polyamide, [CYCA 4]

Rowan Wool Cotton
123 yd. (113 m) per 50 g ball:
50% merino wool, 50% cotton, [CYCA 3]

Sublime Bamboo & Pearls DK
104 yd. (95 m) per 50 g ball:
70% bamboo-sourced viscose,
30% pearl-sourced viscose, [CYCA 3]

Sublime Cashmere Merino Silk Aran
94 yd. (86 m) per 50 g ball:
75% extra-fine merino wool, 20% silk,
5% cashmere, [CYCA 4]

The following yarns are all fancy yarns
from my stash, and I do not have composition
information for all of them. They are used
in the Garland Necklet (p. 18). For this pattern,
gauge is unimportant, and you can mix
and match fancy yarns as you like. Bear in

mind that if you wish to achieve a similar effect in scale, you should use fiber with roughly the same yardage.

Bergere de France Tulle
172 yd. (160 m) per 50 g ball,
[CYCA 4]

Berroco Glacé
75 yd. (69 m) per 50 g hank,
[CYCA 3]

Berroco Metallic FX
85 yd. (78 m) per 25 g hank:
85% rayon, 15% metallic, [CYCA 3]

Colinette Zanziba
103 yd. (94 m) per 100 g hank:
50% wool, 50% rayon, [CYCA 5]

Louisa Harding Sari Ribbon
66 yd. (60 m) per 50 g ball:
90% nylon, 10% metallic, [CYCA 5]

Standard Yarn Weight System

Yarn Weight Symbol and Category Name	Super Fine 1	Fine 2	Light 3	Medium 4	Bulky 5	Super Bulky 6
Types of yarn in category	Sock, fingering, baby	Sport, baby	DK, light worsted	Worsted, afghan, Aran	Chunky, craft, rug	Bulky, roving
Knit gauge range in St st in 4 in.*	27–32 sts	23–26 sts	21–24 sts	16–20 sts	12–15 sts	6–11 sts
Recommended metric needle size	2.25–3.25 mm	3.25–3.75 mm	3.75–4.5 mm	4.5–5.5 mm	5.5–8 mm	8 mm and larger
Recommended U.S. needle size	1–3	3–5	5–7	7–9	9–11	11 and larger
Crochet gauge range in sc in 4 in.*	21–31 sts	16–20 sts	12–17 sts	11–14 sts	8–11 sts	5–9 sts
Recommended metric hook size	2.25–3.5 mm	3.5–4.5 mm	4.5–5.5 mm	5.5–6.5 mm	6.5–9 mm	9 mm and larger
Recommended U.S. hook size	B/1–E/4	E/4–7	7–I/9	I/9–K/10.5	K/10.5–M/13	M/13 and larger

*The information in this table reflects the most commonly used gauges and needle or hook sizes for the specific yarn categories.

Buttons and Trimmings

BEAUTIFUL BUTTONS, FASTENERS, AND TRIMMINGS can add a "wow" factor to any garment. My favorites are made of glass, mother-of-pearl, silver, copper, and ceramic. I'm always on the lookout for unusual handcrafted buttons and love vintage buttons. Also, the idea of recycling old ones from secondhand sweaters bought for practically nothing in thrift shops really appeals to me. I usually prefer shank buttons to those with holes because it's easier to focus on the design of the button.

Color is important when choosing buttons and trimmings, and if you can't get an exact match to the yarn, it's better to go for a complete contrast. Also consider scale when buying buttons. The balance of the garment will be thrown out of kilter if you get this wrong. For example, a bold design in chunky yarn will need big buttons to complement the design, but a fine silk yarn will never look elegant with heavy wooden buttons dragging it down—delicate mother-of-pearl buttons would work better.

Never skimp on trimmings; choose them carefully to complement your shawlette, which has taken lots of your valuable time to knit. If you just can't find what you're looking for, consider making your own. Knots or bobbles will work as fasteners for some projects, and you can always buy button blanks and cover them with knitted fabric.

Knitting Abbreviations

alt   alternate

approx   approximately

beg   beginning

ch   chain (single crochet)

cm   centimeter(s)

cn   cable needle

cont   continue

dec   decrease

ev   every

g   gram(s)

in.   inch(es)

inc   increase

k   knit

k2tog   knit 2 sts together

k3tog   knit 3 sts together

kfb   knit st in front and back

kwise   knitwise

LH   left hand

m   meter(s)

mm   millimeter(s)

p   purl

p2tog   purl 2 sts together

p2tog-b   p1, return this st to LH needle, then with point of RH needle, pass next st over and off needle; then slip st back to RH needle

p3tog   purl 3 sts together

pm   place marker

psso   pass slipped st over

rep   repeat

rem   remaining

RH   right hand

RS   right side

s2kpo   sl2tog kwise, k1, pass 2 slipped sts over

sk   skip

sk2po   slip 1 st wyib, k2tog, psso

skpo   slip 1 st, k1, pass the slipped st over

sl   slip

sl2tog   slip 2 sts together

ssk   (slip, slip, knit)—slip next 2 sts knitwise, one at a time, to RH needle. Insert tip of LH needle into fronts of these sts from left to right and knit them together.

st(s)   stitch(es)

tbl   through back loop

tog   together

w & t   wrap yarn and turn work

WS   wrong side

wyib   with yarn in back

yd.   yard(s)

yo   yarn over needle to make 1 st

Needle and Hook Sizing

Knitting Needles

Millimeter Range	U.S. Size Range
2.25 mm	1
2.75 mm	2
3.25 mm	3
3.5 mm	4
3.75 mm	5
4 mm	6
4.5 mm	7
5 mm	8
5.5 mm	9
6 mm	10
6.5 mm	10½
8 mm	11
9 mm	13
10 mm	15
12.75 mm	17
15 mm	19
19 mm	35
25 mm	50

Crochet Hooks

Millimeter Range	U.S. Size Range
2.25 mm	B-1
2.75 mm	C-2
3.25 mm	D-3
3.5 mm	E-4
3.75 mm	F-5
4 mm	G-6
4.5 mm	7
5 mm	H-8
5.5 mm	I-9
6 mm	J-10
6.5 mm	K-10½
8 mm	L-11
9 mm	M/N-13
10 mm	N/P-15
15 mm	P/Q
16 mm	Q
19 mm	S

Project Index

Madame Alfred Shawlette, p. 10

Kardamili Shawlette, p. 14

Garland Necklet, p. 18

Green at Heart Collar, p. 22

Evergreen Scarf, p. 26

Frost Choker, p. 30

Drift Cowl, p. 36

Penumbra Cowl, p. 38

Enigma Shawl, p. 42

Harlequin Cape, p. 46

Twine Cowl, p. 49

Empty Circle Joined Hat and Scarf, p. 52

Miss Garricks Cowl, p. 58

Arabesque Scarf, p. 62

Bess Ruff, p. 66

Ceilidh Shawlette, p. 70

Purple Patch Shrug, p. 74

Polperro Cape, p. 78

Kitty Capelet, p. 84

Grace Cowl, p. 90

Brontë Fichu, p. 94

Mantilla Shawlette, p. 98

Vamp Boa, p. 102

Treasure Jabot, p. 106

Fizz Capelet, p. 110

Index

About the Author

JEAN MOSS IS ONE OF Britain's leading knit designers. Her innovative combinations of intricate textures, striking colorways, and sophisticated styling have been widely influential in the global knitting community.

A self-taught knitwear designer, Jean produced her own unique collections of handknits for many years, which were sold in the United States, Japan, and Europe. In

the 1980s and 1990s, Jean also worked on design and production for many international fashion houses, such as Polo Ralph Lauren, Laura Ashley, and Benetton. Currently, her designs are featured regularly in *Rowan Knitting and Crochet Magazine, The Knitter*, and *Vogue Knitting,* and for six years she hosted "Ask Jean," an advice column in the U.K. magazine *Knitting.*

Jean is passionate about good design and has always believed that it should be available to all who appreciate it, not just the few who can afford to buy couture. *Sweet Shawlettes* is her 10th book of

handknit designs, the most recent being *In The Mood* and *Wandering Spirits* for Araucania Yarns.

Jean's other passions include gardening, music, and vegetarian food. Her personal take on color, texture, shape, and form is expressed in the one-off, imaginative gardens she designs for clients in North Yorkshire, England. Music plays a big part in her life, and her album *More Yarn Will Do the Trick* is a trio of textile-related songs.

For the past decade, Jean and her partner, Philip, have hosted knitting and garden tours in the United Kingdom, which have become so successful that they are now going further afield to exotic locations such as Morocco and Greece. She loves to meet other knitters and travels extensively, teaching workshops in both the United States and Europe. For more information on Jean's books, patterns, kits, ready-to-wear, workshops, lectures, and tours, visit www.jeanmoss.com.